Google Plus First Look: a tip-packed, comprehensive look at Google+

Get up and running with Google+ fast

Ralph Roberts

BIRMINGHAM - MUMBAI

Google Plus First Look:
a tip-packed, comprehensive look at Google+

First published: November 2011

Production Reference: 1181111

Published by Packt Publishing Ltd.
Livery Place
35 Livery Street
Birmingham B3 2PB, UK.

ISBN 978-1-84968-534-4

www.packtpub.com

Cover Image by Artie Ng (artherng@yahoo.com.au)

Credits

Author
Ralph Roberts

Reviewers
David Broschinsky
Amol Y. Datar

Acquisition Editor
Dilip Venkatesh

Development Editor
Shreerang Deshpande

Technical Editor
Llewellyn F. Rozario

Copy Editor
Neha Shetty

Project Coordinator
Joel Goveya

Proofreader
Samantha Lyon

Indexer
Rekha Nair

Production Coordinator
Arvindkumar Gupta
Aparna Bhagat

Cover Work
Arvindkumar Gupta
Aparna Bhagat

About the Author

Ralph Roberts is a decorated Vietnam veteran and worked with NASA during the Apollo moon program. He built his first personal computer in 1976 and has been writing about them, and on them, since his first published article *"Down with Typewriters"* in 1978. He has written over 100 books along with thousands of articles and short stories. His best sellers include the first U.S. book on computer viruses (which resulted in several appearances on national TV) and Classic Cooking with Coca-Cola®, a cookbook that has been in continuous print for the past 17 years and sold half a million copies. He is also a video producer with over 100 DVD titles now for sale nationally on places such as Amazon.com. He has also produced hundreds of hours of video for local TV in the Western North Carolina area and sold scripts to Hollywood producers. Previously for Packt, Ralph wrote *Celtx: Open Source Screenwriting and Google App Inventor*. Ralph and his wife Pat live on a farm in the mountains of Western North Carolina with two horses.

Thanks to my wife, Pat, for her superior proofing.

To the wonderful people at Packt, especially Dilip Venkatesh, and my most astute and encouraging editor, Joel Goveya.

To all the kind folks on Google+ and all the new friends I am making there.

About the Reviewers

David Broschinsky has a passion for technology and helping individuals use technology to improve their lives. He has worked in the computer industry for over 20 years with a focus on user experience. He currently runs his own User Experience consultancy, Usable Patterns, in Salt Lake City, UT where he enjoys working with mature companies and small startups.

Amol Datar has worked for Courion IT Pvt. Ltd as a QA lead. He completed his MCS from Pune University. He is a cool person and loves to listen to the opinion of others before making an appropriate decision. He loves challenges in life and also appreciates like-minded people.

He's been having a great journey for more than 6 years in the IT industry.

He is a die-hard Manchester United (Manu-Red devils) fan, loves to watch cricket matches, be it domestic, club match or International cricket.

It has been excellent experience for him to work with companies such as Siemens Information Systems Ltd (SISL-Mumbai), UK – Royal Bank of Scotland (Onsite), Dell – Pune, Cybage software.

I'd like to thank my wife, Priya Datar, who has inspired me to take up book reviewing.

Also, my special thanks to Shreerang Deshpande, who has provided me the opportunity to review this book on Google Plus.

www.PacktPub.com

Support files, eBooks, discount offers and more

You might want to visit www.PacktPub.com for support files and downloads related to your book.

Did you know that Packt offers eBook versions of every book published, with PDF and ePub files available? You can upgrade to the eBook version at www.PacktPub.com and as a print book customer, you are entitled to a discount on the eBook copy. Get in touch with us at service@packtpub.com for more details.

At www.PacktPub.com, you can also read a collection of free technical articles, sign up for a range of free newsletters and receive exclusive discounts and offers on Packt books and eBooks.

http://PacktLib.PacktPub.com

Do you need instant solutions to your IT questions? PacktLib is Packt's online digital book library. Here, you can access, read and search across Packt's entire library of books.

Why Subscribe?

- Fully searchable across every book published by Packt
- Copy and paste, print and bookmark content
- On demand and accessible via web browser

Free Access for Packt account holders

If you have an account with Packt at www.PacktPub.com, you can use this to access PacktLib today and view nine entirely free books. Simply use your login credentials for immediate access.

Instant Updates on New Packt Books

Get notified! Find out when new books are published by following @PacktEnterprise on Twitter, or the *Packt Enterprise* Facebook page.

Table of Contents

Preface

In four years on Facebook, I gained 453 friends. In four months on Google+, I have 10,141 followers. In the course of this book, you'll learn everything I know about G+ and have a bunch of fun doing it!

At first glance, **Google+** (or **Plus**, the terms are interchangeable) seems awfully familiar. You can make **Posts**, like on Facebook's Wall. The **Stream**—a continuous page of posts from your friends—looks like Facebook's News Feed. That little **+1** button on Plus is much the same as Facebook's **Like** button (and perhaps where the name for Plus came from).

Here's what my Plus profile page looks like currently (as this book goes to press):

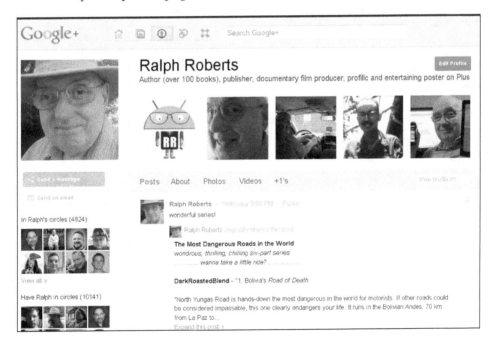

Points of similarity to FB and other social media networks do not end as described above. Early reviewers remind me of the classic poem about the blind men and the elephant. One took hold of its trunk and said an elephant is like a hose. Another felt its leg and said an elephant is mighty like a tree. And so forth.

About Plus, one writer says it's a "Facebook" killer, another that with the Plus **Following** feature it's more like Twitter than Twitter (but more powerful), and yet another compares it to the digital media **haven|Tumblr**, because of its ease in sharing photos and videos.

Truth is, Google+ is all this and a good deal more. It's a redesign of social and business contact management using the latest web techniques. And it has a lot going for it, but there is one bit of magic rising above the rest and causing so many of us to come running (over ten million in its first two weeks of limited availability). That magic is **Circles**!

Because many already see the genius of Google's real offering — Plus is a new beginning! A chance to "reboot" our social life and to better manage all those hundreds of friends on Facebook. We have absolutely no idea who these hundreds of friends are, but their posts clutter our News Feeds.

Circles give us the ability to organize all our contacts into groups. So instead of having a huge mass of "friends" (most of whom you have no idea who they are), you have incredibly more manageable groups such as the ones Plus starts you with — *Friends, Acquaintances, Family,* and *Following* (people whose posts you wish to follow, but not interact with, like on Twitter).

You can add all the additional Circles you like. One for each club you belong to, people you went to school with, another for those you work with — the possibilities are endless.

However, as already stated, there are many more attractions. This book:

- Gives you an exciting but comprehensive first look at the features of Google+ and how to best use them.

- Shows the best ways of rebooting your social networks using the power of Plus.

- Displays numerous examples of what you use social networking for and how to do it in ways that work and do not offend.

- Explores ways of promoting yourself, a product, your company, a cause, and so on. The right way, effectively and inoffensively.

- And a lot more!

What this book covers

Chapter 1, Joining Plus and What to Do First. This chapter introduces that excitement and how you can best join, and the kind of initial setup that guarantees a successful and fun-filled experience.

In it, we will:

- Take look at the advantages of Plus
- See how to join and do it
- Discuss privacy concerns
- Set up our profiles (yes, we'll want more than one).

Chapter 2, Sorting Everyone in to Circles. We will:

- Learn how Circles work and their tremendous advantages
- Set up our first Circles for Friends, Acquaintances, and Family
- Decide who we want to follow and learn how to do so
- Master easy dragging and dropping in maintaining our Circles
- Create and use new types of Circles beyond the standard ones

It's easy to add friends. Thumbnail photos are generated from your regular Google profile so if a photo is not attached to that yet, we won't see you. Not everyone will have a thumbnail ID yet, as shown in the following screenshot:

Chapter 3, Hanging Out. Other social media systems are adding video chat and related features. Plus was designed from the ground up with these fun and powerful things built in!

In this chapter, we will see (literally see) how Hangouts work.

- What Hangouts are and how we use them
- Setting up a webcam or other video input
- Joining existing Hangouts
- Creating your own Hangouts

Here I am checking my hair (uh huh) and preparing to hang out:

Chapter 4, Streaming. Two major topics join us in this chapter — Streams and Sparks.

In this chapter it's time to:

- Practice Posting to the Stream and determine how to drill down so that each Post goes to the right audience
- Learn how to control what we see and when we see it (as opposed to all those zillions of posts you're not interested in but which make you miss the good stuff on other social networks)

Chapter 5, Sharing Media. Plus gives us powerful built-in features for sharing photos, videos, animated `gifs`, and so on. We'll enjoy learning those in this chapter.

So here we:

- Select and prepare photos for uploading
- Upload and caption photos
- Select and prepare videos
- Upload and caption videos
- Learn how to share to your various Circles or make public

Chapter 6, Mobile and Games. In today's world of smartphones, we take our social networks with us.

Together, we will be:

- Finding the right app for your phone or tablet computer
- Learning how to keep up with Circles, and so on, on the mobile device
- Posting from your phone
- Uploading photos and videos from your phone or other device

This is what Plus looks like on the free Android app (iPhone and others no charge too):

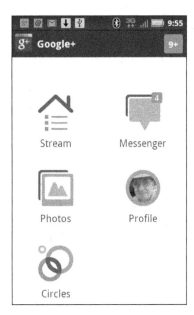

Chapter 7, Promoting on Plus the Right Way. Many people use social media, like Facebook, to promote themselves, their company, their organization, or a cause. This is fine as long as we do it right and don't offend anyone. If people get irritated by your actions, then they won't pay attention to you.

In this chapter, we learn to do it right, politely, and effectively by knowing about:

- Netiquette, what it is, and why you should use it
- Setting up accounts for a business or organization
- Advertising without it looking like an ad
- Marketing politely, but in an interesting manner that works
- Networking with others
- Starting groups

Appendix. This chapter provides helpful websites and other resources.

What you need for this book

The only thing required (aside from a computer and/or smartphone) is a Google account, which is free. In Chapter 1, we'll see how to sign up, if you don't already have an account.

Who this book is for

Just as Google+ is for everyone, so too is this book. Plus is meant not to be a standalone social network, but an integral part of Google's other offerings such as Google search, Gmail, YouTube, Picasa, and so forth. As we'll see, they all work together.

And Plus is also for everyone, in that there are so many fun and exciting ways of using it, as we'll experience in the coming pages. So let's get to it.

Conventions

In this book, you will find a number of styles of text that distinguish between different kinds of information. Here are some examples of these styles, and an explanation of their meaning.

Code words in text are shown as follows: "We can include other contexts through the use of the `include` directive."

New terms and **important words** are shown in bold. Words that you see on the screen, in menus or dialog boxes for example, appear in the text like this: "Choose a photo from your computer and upload it by clicking on **change photo**.".

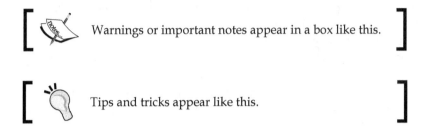

> Warnings or important notes appear in a box like this.

> Tips and tricks appear like this.

Reader feedback

Feedback from our readers is always welcome. Let us know what you think about this book—what you liked or may have disliked. Reader feedback is important for us to develop titles that you really get the most out of.

To send us general feedback, simply send an e-mail to feedback@packtpub.com, and mention the book title via the subject of your message.

If there is a book that you need and would like to see us publish, please send us a note in the **SUGGEST A TITLE** form on www.packtpub.com or e-mail suggest@packtpub.com.

If there is a topic that you have expertise in and you are interested in either writing or contributing to a book, see our author guide on www.packtpub.com/authors.

Customer support

Now that you are the proud owner of a Packt book, we have a number of things to help you to get the most from your purchase.

Errata

Although we have taken every care to ensure the accuracy of our content, mistakes do happen. If you find a mistake in one of our books—maybe a mistake in the text or the code—we would be grateful if you would report this to us. By doing so, you can save other readers from frustration and help us improve subsequent versions of this book. If you find any errata, please report them by visiting http://www.packtpub. com/support, selecting your book, clicking on the **errata submission form** link, and entering the details of your errata. Once your errata are verified, your submission will be accepted and the errata will be uploaded on our website, or added to any list of existing errata, under the Errata section of that title. Any existing errata can be viewed by selecting your title from http://www.packtpub.com/support.

Piracy

Piracy of copyright material on the Internet is an ongoing problem across all media. At Packt, we take the protection of our copyright and licenses very seriously. If you come across any illegal copies of our works, in any form, on the Internet, please provide us with the location address or website name immediately so that we can pursue a remedy.

Please contact us at copyright@packtpub.com with a link to the suspected pirated material.

We appreciate your help in protecting our authors, and our ability to bring you valuable content.

Questions

You can contact us at questions@packtpub.com if you are having a problem with any aspect of the book, and we will do our best to address it.

1
Joining Plus and What to Do First

Ever wish you could completely start over? Begin an entirely new online life? Well, as far as social media goes, that time is now.

And the time could not be better! Everything from interaction with your friends, to communications with coworkers and clients, professional contacts and development, meeting those who share your hobbies, and so much more now depends on social networking. **Google+** is the fastest growing and, arguably, the easiest to learn.

If you're already using Facebook, for example, then one of the big attractions of **Plus** is starting out fresh. Creating your friends lists in a controllable manner, making online interaction more manageable, and enjoying the power of a completely new software. All free, by the way.

Google+ or (as most of us seem to be calling it) **Google Plus** gives us all of the above and more.

This chapter introduces that excitement and shows how to join Plus. It also gives you the kind of painless initial setup that guarantees a successful and fun-filled experience for years to come.

So let's:

- Learn what Google Plus is and does
- Take a look at the advantages of Plus
- See how to join
- Discuss privacy concerns
- Set up our profiles
- And above all, learn just why Google+ is the place to be!

We begin with just exactly what Google Plus is.

What is Plus?

Google Plus (or Google+) is a brand-new social media network using all the latest in web software.

Google is one of the giants on the Internet, dominant in search engines and other areas, but was never the type of all-inclusive social media that Plus aims to be (which has been most recently ruled by Facebook). Many members, as well as myself, feel Plus is a game changer.

Plus is not Google's first attempt at social networking (we'll be nice and not mention Buzz and Wave). However, they have had successes. Their **orkut** network, popular in Europe, has over 15 million members. And, of course, YouTube — the master of video sites — is Google's.

For those of us keeping score at home, `ebizmba.com` (a business-oriented site), listed in the top fifteen social media networks for August, 2011. Not surprisingly, Facebook (with over 700 million users) was the leader. Twitter was second. Myspace, once the king, has fallen to fourth.

Google Plus — which only started in June, 2011, and is still in an early growth stage — was already up to 6th with over 32 million members as I started this book. Now it's around 50 million. And those members have posted over a billion items! I've added a fair share of that myself.

So, yes, Plus looks like it's very popular and can continue its fast growth (that's pretty much an understatement, I believe). Here's what the entry page looks like (`https://plus.google.com`):

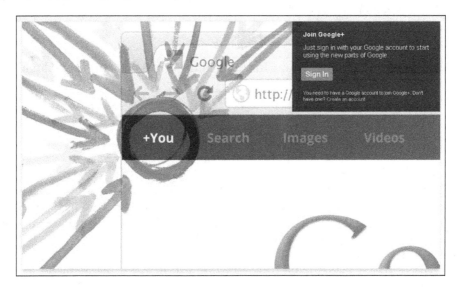

We'll discuss the procedure for joining Plus in just a moment. As we prep this book for publication, Plus is now open for the public, so invitations (as was true during the beta programs) are no longer required. Just join. It's completely free.

Plus provides several advantages that ensure rapid growth aside from all the new designs and powerful web software. Not least of which is its close integration with other Google products, especially Gmail.

Gmail is Google's free e-mail service that already has over 200 million users worldwide. Plus runs (at least partially) on top of the Gmail system. When I check my Gmail, in the upper-right corner it tells me how many Plus notifications are waiting for me, as shown in the following screenshot. A click opens those up.

I also get notifications in e-mails, as shown in the following screenshot:

Additionally, there's a link to your Plus page in the upper-left corner of Gmail:

The close integration of Google+ with Gmail (and other Google products, as we see in this book) makes using Plus easier and more powerful. There are also apps for the popular type of smartphones (such as My Droid 2) that let us keep track and interact no matter where we might be.

Back to what Plus is. Social media runs the gamut from terse 140-character messages like Twitter to the vastness of Facebook (current leader after supplanting MySpace and now, obviously, a target in its own right).

Like Facebook, Google+ falls more toward the *"do everything for you"* end. Unlike Facebook, Plus is not stuck with a lot of legacy code. Plus is (as already stated) an up-to-date, innovative, and new social network built from the ground up and designed for both great power and ease-of-use.

Features of Plus

We introduced some of the major features in the *Preface* and showed them in the illustration of the main Plus entry screen (the first image in this chapter). However, let's review the major ones:

- **Circles**: The hot new concept that, by itself, puts Plus above all other social media networks. By the use of Circles (you can have as many as you like), you can categorize friends, family, acquaintances, people at work, schoolmates, members of the hiking club, or any of the many other groupings in your life. Takes all the confusion out of social interaction! We'll run around in ... err... circles in the next chapter. The introduction to Circles from the Plus website is shown in the following screenshot:

- **Stream**: A newsfeed that is somewhat similar to Facebook's, but much more controllable because you can select which circle to see posts from, and so on.

- **Hangouts**: A video chat service where, using a cheap USB camera, you can both see and talk to your friends. The following screenshot shows how Plus introduces it on the Plus site:

- **Chat** : Standard text chats and a feature called **Messenger** that allows us to gather several friends together for a group chat from our smartphones.

There are other nice features, all of which we'll master in this book. For example, photos and videos (both yours and of the people in your circles post) are easy to upload and share.

If you have a smartphone with the Google Plus app on it (free from the Plus site), photos on the phone automatically upload to your private photo albums. Share what you wish, when you wish. No one else can see them until you do. This feature is called **Instant Upload**. For those concerned with privacy and if this action bothers them, I'll show you how to turn that feature off later in the book (it's in the settings of the official Google+ app).

Additional features are under development, such as **Games** and **Questions**. If they appear before I've finished this book, then we will see what they do.

Breaking news: Wow, the wait for **Games** was not all that long, they are here now! Literally overnight from when I wrote the preceding paragraph. We'll cover **Games** later in this book:

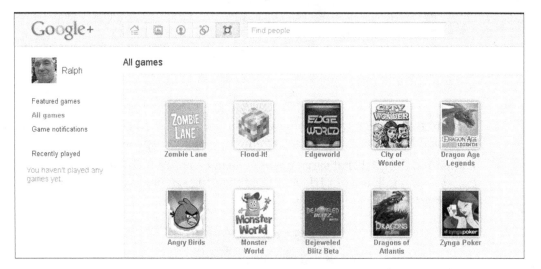

The **Games** icon is already in place now on the Google+ control bar, as shown in the following screenshot:

Furthermore, later in this book is a chapter on how to promote on Plus. Promotion is a very exciting and important concept. We all have something we want others to know, whether it is only the fact that we are jolly good fellows and fun to know or that we make our living by selling products, or services, or by pushing for a good cause—for whatever reason, promotion is important and Plus makes it easy.

Often when we meet someone new, one of the first questions they ask is *"What do you do for a living?"* Soon enough, you might answer, *"I post stuff on Google Plus."*

The following is an example where I share this breaking news with all the people who have me in their circles to make sure they know I'm writing a book about Plus (which will result, we would hope) in increased book sales.

This is how I make my living, got to keep my computers fed. By the way, thank you for buying this book, truly appreciated.

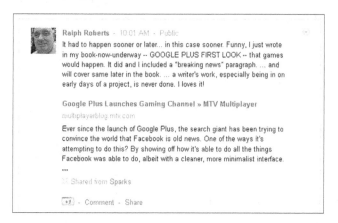

Continuing, Vic Gundotra—Senior Vice President for Social at Google—in an interview published by **Mashable** (mashable.com) says Google+ is *"designed to be an improvement to all of Google."*

Vic goes on to add that this is why the Google's navigation bar on the main Google search page (as shown in the following screenshot) now shows a link to Plus and any notifications you might have waiting (a white number in a small red box, just click on it).

Now we're beginning to get a feeling of what Plus is (and there will be much more coming). The next question becomes why would we want to join?

Why join Google Plus?

The rationale for beginning any new activity fall in two categories, and social media's no exception.

First, we have the technical. How does this benefit me? Is it easy to upload photos and videos? To make comments? To control which people I interact with? Does it make live chats with my friends easier? And so on and so forth.

The good news is that the answer to all of the above questions is 'yes'. The preceding section introduced us to that and throughout the rest of this book we will be learning and using all those neat features on Google Plus.

However, as exciting and interesting as Plus makes them, technical goodies are not enough. We need the second category to close the deal.

These are *of the heart* reasons, because life is so much more than just colorful graphics on a computer screen.

Ask yourself the following questions:

- Is using Plus exciting?
- Do I find satisfaction and enjoyment in the ways it allows me to interact with people?
- Will my friends enjoy it and want to be on it with me?
- Above all, is it a satisfying activity I enjoy and which meets my needs on many levels — some of which I may not even know exist or that I've been missing input on?

That answer is also a resounding yes! We will see and experience examples throughout, but here are a few examples of how social media in general, and Plus in particular, fulfills human needs. These can be, and I hope will be, benefits received from joining and participating on Google Plus. While the same applies to other social media (hence their great popularity), Plus makes these things even easier.

Here are a few of those reasons to get us started:

1. **Social contacts**: You could hang out at a local bar, meet three drunks and eat stale peanuts. Or from your own comfy chair, in the warm light of your own computer screen, you can eat fresh peanuts while meeting dozens or even hundreds of interesting people from all over the world every evening. Seriously, the more people we interact with, the more interesting life becomes. Being social generates warmth and a sense of wellbeing in our lives.

2. **Groups**: Broaden your horizons. Be a part of all sorts of groups and meet all levels of folks. Control what groups you're conversing with and when. That's what the Circles feature is all about.

3. **Cheap**: Did I mention it was free? Well, it's free.

4 . **Entertaining**: When you get right down to it, people (all of us) like people. Interesting characters, wise cracks, kindred spirits, tellers of truly funny jokes and wise sayings, and ever so many more, all of which Plus streams by for our enjoyment.

5 . **Community**: A community is a (large or small) grouping of people with a common interest. Perhaps they live in the same geographic location, or share the same political viewpoint, or love the same sports team. Plus lets you join together with like-minded friends for discussion, to follow events, entertainment, and all the other good stuff members of communities give each other.

6. **Connection**: Keep in touch daily, weekly, or whatever interval pleases you with friends, acquaintances, family, and more. They could live down the street or on another continent, but you can remain close to them on your computer or smartphone.

7 . **Sharing**: Photos, videos, recipes, what Junior did and how darn cute it was, and a million other things can all be shared with friends, fellow workers, and many others, in any mix of your Circles.

8. **Family**: Communicating, supporting, and loving our family and other relatives keeps us together, and is one of the most rewarding things we can do. Post a message to mom tonight.

9. **Career**: Keeping up with co-workers, others in your vocation or profession, or even finding employment if you're between jobs, all of it is possible on Plus.

10. **Promotion**: Marketing your company, your talents, and more is another great way to use social media like Plus (and we'll show you how to do it the right way).

11. **Hobbies and Interests**: Groups of folks and individual friends who share your hobby and other interests are easy to find and communicate with on Plus.

12. **Personal Improvement**: Above all, as we interact and learn, we grow. Plus keeps your mind agile and interested.

To sum up this sampling of reasons to join this great social media network, consider the following screenshot from the Plus site:

See the red circle with all the arrows pointing to it? Yes, this network might very well be named **+You** instead of Google+.

Okay, ready to join? Good, let's see how.

How to join Plus

First, you need a Google account, which is free, gives you Gmail (Google's e-mail service), and access to a growing number of Google applications on the web. Having Gmail is essential because of the integration between it and Plus for sending you notifications of posts and other events.

Here's the way you get all that.

Getting a Google Account

If you do not have a Google account yet, it's simple enough to get one. Free, of course.

 Google currently encourages you to use your real name on Plus, so you'll need to register that way (they have been deleting Plus accounts which do not meet this criteria). We'll discuss privacy concerns and this controversial policy later in this chapter and explain more about real names, pro and con.

To register, carry out the following steps:

1. Browse to `https://www.google.com/accounts/NewAccount` (the sign-up page is as shown in the following screenshot).

2. Fill out the form to create your account and you are good to go. Again, it's free.

Here's how the registration page looks:

Complete the application (using your real name). For example, my Gmail address is `ralph.roberts@gmail.com`. If your name is Bob Smith, you might wind up with `BobSmith426@gmail.com` or something similar. Don't worry. The Plus application system guides you through choosing your real name (which is required).

Once you have a Google account, which includes a Gmail account (like mine, as follows) take a little time to explore Gmail and the other Google apps that are now yours (some of which we see listed on the top line in the following screenshot):

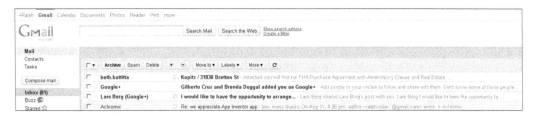

Calendar, for example, is a sophisticated appointments calendar easily shared with others. My wife and I use this daily. All our appointments are available not only on our computers, but also on our Droids. If one of us makes a change, then it shows up on the other's phone; a great and convenient way to sync our lives and activities. The other apps are quite useful too.

Of course, our book is not about Gmail or the many Google apps opened to us by having a Google account.

However, Gmail is important as it serves as one of our gateways into Google Plus. Note the **+Ralph** menu item in the extreme upper-left corner, as shown in the preceding screenshot. Once you've joined Plus, your Gmail will have that too. Clicking on it takes you to your Plus home page, and there is a small box over on the far right of the menu bar that is red, if you have notifications, with the numbers of items to look. If there are no pending notifications, the box is gray.

However, more than just a handy link, Gmail lets us interact with Plus right in our e-mails. Let's take, as an example, the notification I just received, as shown in the following screenshot:

Plus notifies me via e-mail that two people have added me to their circles, meaning I see whatever they post that's tagged as `Public`.

Now comes an important difference between Plus and Facebook, as well as other social media networks. Instead of one big blob of hundreds of friends, we can control where or even if we add folks to our circles.

In the preceding case, I can click on the thumbnails because not everyone has a profile picture and some use graphics like Gilberto's. In checking, I find Gilberto is already in my Interesting Folks circle (a custom circle I created just for keeping up with posts that appear of people worth following). I know who Brenda is and she went into my App Inventor circle because we share that interest.

Again, all the ways of setting up and maintaining Circles are in the next chapter. Please let me emphasize again that the concept of Circles, which is a stroke of Google genius, sets Plus apart from all other social networks to date, giving us the ability of categorizing and thus, controlling our contacts.

To summarize this section, you need a Google account and you need to use Gmail, all of which is free.

Getting a Plus Membership

When I started writing this book, Google Plus membership was **Limited** to **By invitation only**. It is now open to the public.

If you have a Gmail account, you can start using Plus immediately. Just log in to Gmail and click on the Plus button on the upper-left of the screen (the **+** symbol followed by your first name).

If you do not have a Gmail account, see the preceding section on how to create one.

Now, we move on to the real names requirement.

Privacy concerns

In a requirement that has generated some controversy, Google insists on real names instead of pseudonyms, as people use on many websites to hide their identity. One of the reasons for this is that Google wants users to have verified identities, both privately and publically.

Here's the start of how Google expresses this policy, as follows (see http://www.google.com/support/+/bin/answer.py?answer=1228271):

Using real names is an attempt to (as Google states in the preceding material) make the site more like the real world, where you can find people based on the name you know them by. It also cuts down on nastiness and incivility (flame wars) often seen on sites where individuals hide behind concocted user or screen names.

This is not an unusual concept. Facebook started out by suggesting that real names be used and this is still very common on that network.

In the long run, it's quite possible that, due to pressure, Google will relax this policy. I suspect this will eventually be the case, but for the time being, use your real name or risk getting kicked off. That's the way it is.

Personally, I've been on the Internet pretty much continuously for decades and always used my real name, and will keep on doing that. As a writer, I make my living by having people know who I am.

I realize others have privacy concerns about putting their real names on the Internet, so you'll have to make your own choice in this matter.

Mine is: Real names are okay and Plus is fantastic.

Profiles

Speaking of revealing stuff, you can put as much or as little in your **Profile** as you like (some of which is asked during the join-up process). I have not done much on my profile, so let's use me as an example and get it filled up. Some of this will come from the already completed Google profile that is required before sign-up. To edit:

1. On your Google Plus home page, click on your photo (or where the photo goes).

2. When the profile page comes up, click on **Edit Profile** and you get the following page:

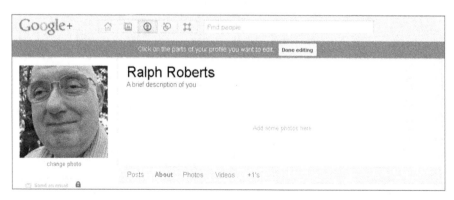

3. Choose a photo from your computer and upload it by clicking on **change photo**.

4. Now we need a description. Being a writer, I have no trouble in coming up with a lot more than will display easily. However, keep it short here, there's more space coming up for the long bio.

5. Next, we add some photos (just anything you'd like to share). Click on **Add some photos here**. I've uploaded a few that were handy on my computer, but I'll soon add some of the mountain scenery and waterfalls that I love photographing. Here's what my profile looks like so far:

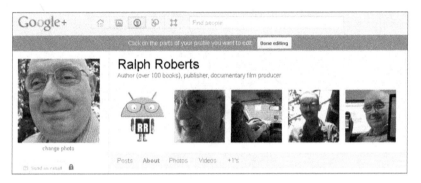

Following is a description of us and the photos. We can add more biographical information to both, help people be sure they've found the right person, and just read interesting stuff about you. Following is what the form looks like, just click on each item to fill it out. As with the photos and everything else, you can change them whenever you like and as much as you want.

It is possible to have more than one profile, that displays certain elements of your bio display only to the circles you wish it to. This is the way that works.

As you save each bio item about yourself, a drop-down menu, as shown in the following screenshot, asks you about the people who you want to make that viewable to. This lets you structure your bio so that different groups see things pertinent to them.

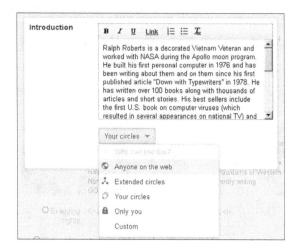

We'll revisit setting up your profile for specific purposes later in the book.

What we learned

We've learned what Google Plus is and what it does, took a good look at the advantages of using Plus, and found out how to join the site. We discussed the real name issue and set up our profile. And above all, saw just why Google+ is the place to be!

Now, time to explore Circles and get set up for the best and most enjoyable experience of using Google Plus!

2
Sorting Everyone into Circles

It's a stroke of genius that, according to many who are already on Plus (including myself) makes Plus a shoo-in to become the next major social media home for hundreds of millions of folks. That's **Circles**!

Instead of having this great mass of friends in one big unmanageable blob as in other online social media sites, Plus lets us manage them in small, easy to understand groups. You can create as many of these as you like (later in this chapter, I'll show you some examples of that and show you how to plan and set up your own).

I love Circles! It's just so beautifully simple when you grasp what they are and you'll enjoy them a lot.

In this chapter, we will:

- Learn the basics of using Plus
- Learn how Circles work and their tremendous advantages
- Set up our first circles for Friends, Acquaintances, and Family
- Decide who we want to follow and learn how to do so
- Master easy dragging and dropping in maintaining our circles
- Create and use new types of Circles beyond the standard ones

This is how the Plus site introduces Circles on its site:

Circles

You share different things with different people. But sharing the right stuff with the right people shouldn't be a hassle. Circles makes it easy to put your friends from Saturday night in one circle, your parents in another, and your boss in a circle by himself, just like real life.

This chapter is how I introduce Circles and, together, we'll rapidly and easily gain skill in using this key feature of Plus.

But, first, if you guys are anything like me, you're already playing around on Plus and already have a few people in your circles. This is a good thing, so let's look at some shortcuts. These are simple tips that make your user experience even more enjoyable.

Tips on using Plus

When I originally wrote this, I read (on Google Plus, of course) an article that said 48 percent of those 32 million and growing members of Plus have not yet posted anything! Now (as I do the final proof on this book) that figure is over 50 million and growing rapidly (according to Paul Allen who tracks and posts this on Plus) as Google+ is open to the public, but the percentage of members not posting articles probably still remains the same.

Sooner or later, however, you (and many of them) will want to post stuff. After all sharing comments, links, photos, videos, and so on is the basic concept and feature of most social networks and communication. Here are some methods of enhancing your posts.

How to post

First, we need to know the mechanics of posting comments on Plus.

To practice posting, begin on your home page of Plus by clicking on a circle under the **Stream** heading. I've created one named Sandbox to play in and not irritate folks while I test various features of posting. No one sees this circle but me and, okay, you guys reading this book.

At the top of the big middle column in any circle's stream is a comment box, all grayed out as shown in the following screenshot:

 A new feature lets you e-mail a person directly from their profile. Click on the person's name to bring up their profile, and then click on the e-mail link below their profile photo.

Click anywhere in the preceding comment box and it expands as here, ready to accept whatever we wish to post:

Let's look first at the icons available in the comment textbox.

Ignore the I-beam cursor on the left; that just shows us where to start typing. Clicking on the **x** in the top-right cancels the post at any time as long we don't click on the **Share** button.

Now, the four small icons in the lower-right:

1. **Camera icon** - The small, green icon, leftmost of the four icons, allows us to add photographs, make albums of several photos, and include photographs from your phone (you'll want to download the Google+ app onto your phone in order to be able to do that).

Clicking on **Add photos** opens a directory dialog box on your computer and you can simply drag-and-drop photos from your computer into your post, as shown in the following screenshot:

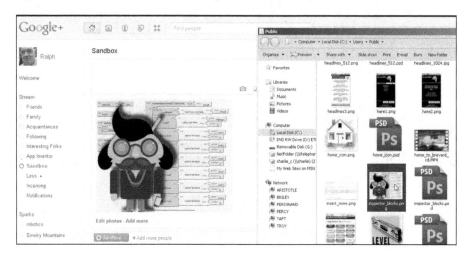

2. **Video icon**: The little screen with a red play button (second from left of the four icons in the post-entry textbox) lets us upload videos from our computer (drag-and-drop as above), or from YouTube (Google owns YouTube, interfacing is easy), or from our phone.

You can also just cut and paste photo and video web links.

3. **Link icon**: (Looks like a little paperclip on its side) This is for including links to web pages. Clicking on it gives us an entry box as shown in the following screenshot:

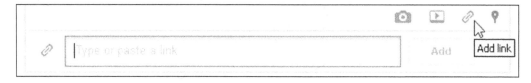

The nice thing about including web links in your posts is the excitement Plus adds by automatically including a slide show of the graphics on that page. For example, if you're making a comment about those unusual statues on Easter Island, a link to the Wikipedia article about Easter Island adds a lot of visual appeal, as follows:

4. **Place icon**: Adds our location by clicking on the small map marker pin, allowing people to click on it in your post and be connected to Google Maps. However, it's not very accurate (the following address is approximately six miles from where I am). I'm sure an editing feature will be added sometime so that this location tag can be made more accurate.

Once you've added all you desire to your post, it's time to choose who sees it. Below the post textbox will be a blue button with the name of the circle you are presently in.

Doing nothing except clicking on the **Share** button publishes your post, but only members of this one circle (who've added your circle to those they watch) can see it.

If you want your other circles to see it, click on **Add more people** (next to the blue button) and a menu like the following pops up. Select the desired circles and click on **Share**.

And here's some more ways to make your post pop out at readers.

Text emphasis

Used in moderation, typeface styles such as bold, italic, and strikeout (see examples in the following screenshot) add much to posts, calling out points of emphasis, adding humor, and so forth.

Adding these type styles in a post is easy, this is how:

1. **Bold** - Enclose the word or words to be emboldened between two asterisks like this *a bold statement*

2. **Italic** - Italicize by using the underscore character like: _it really happened_

3. **Strikethrough** - A strikethrough is done by adding a hyphen before and after. It is often used to impart humor such as: I ~~kicked my computer across the room~~ decided to vigorously reboot my machine

The use of type styles in posts, as we see above, is easy and definitely will do much to set us apart from the majority of posters.

Editing and deleting

Another way of putting up distinctive posts that reflect well on you is correcting typos!

Mistakes, misstatements, or just being downright sloppy makes us look bad. Not that I'd ever write sloppily, not often anyway. However, when I do, I edit it out and no one sees it.

Using typos, misspellings, and unclear language in the points we're trying to put forth just makes us look stupid. We are not stupid.

Most of our posts are what, ten or twelve words maybe? (That is by no means the limit; you can have quite long posts if you like.) Read them over and make corrections before hitting the **Share** button. However, what if you do not see the mistake until after it's posted? No problem. Just click on the little gray downward-pointing arrow in a circle in the upper-right corner of your post, as shown in the following screenshot, and a drop-down menu appears. In the example here, I am editing the post with typeface styles in it as related in the preceding section.

The four choices in the drop-down menu are as follows:

1. **Edit this post**: Allows us to fix typos, correct spelling, add more sentences or paragraphs, and so on. And, of course, only you can make changes in your post.

2. **Delete this post**: Click here to remove the post entirely, which can be done now or months later.

3. **Disable comments**: If you want to stop people from commenting on your posts, this menu selection makes that possible. Clicking on the selection changes it to **Enable comments** so that later, should you so decide, the post can again accept comments. Try this out and watch one of your published posts. The **Comment** selection will appear and disappear depending on whether you've disabled or enabled comments.

4. **Lock this post**: This allows us to toggle the ability of others to share our posts into other circles (ones we do not belong to). Also, try this out and watch one of your published posts—the **Share** selection will appear and disappear depending on whether you've disabled or enabled sharing.

The above, of course, is for our posts, but what about other people's posts? What can we do about them?

Other people's posts

First, what if you're getting too many posts from one person and you're not really interested in them?

Two choices: Remove (delete) him or her from your circles (and all their posts disappear from your stream), or move them into a `catch all` circle that you only look at when the mood strikes you. More about that later in the chapter, but here's what we are able to do with individual posts.

Remember that little downward arrow in the gray circle that opened the drop-down menu in your posts? It's there in post from others as well. Click on it and we get the following menu:

Here's what these four choices do:

1. **Link to this post**: Clicking on this choice turns the post into a separate web page. Copy the URL in the address window of your browser, as shown in the following screenshot, and you can post it anywhere. You can post it in your blog, tweet it, send it in e-mails, and so on. Or you can also just click on the timestamp on the post. This is called a permalink, or a permanent link.

2. **Report abuse**: See something you find offensive or contrary to the rules of Plus? Report it by clicking on this choice, checking the reason, and clicking on **Submit**.

3. **Mute this post**: Hides post from site but leaves it in place. Undoing the mute by clicking on **Undo mute**, as shown in the following screenshot, makes the post visible again.

4. **Block this person**: First, my apologies to Trey for using him as an example. I didn't really block you, Trey! Trey's in my **Interesting Persons** circle and I enjoy his posts. However, this is the dialog you get if you are really blocking someone.

While we're looking at other people's posts, here are some shortcut keys providing an even more enjoyable viewing and reading experience.

Shortcuts

Get in the habit of using these keyboard shortcuts, they save time and effort:

1. In a stream, hit the *space* key on your keyboard to go down the stream of posts, one screen at a time. Use *shift+space* to go up.

2. Hit *j* to go down one post at a time and *k* takes you up one post.

3. While using these shortcuts, tap the *Enter* key and a comment box opens up above as in this post I wanted to comment on by my friend, Bobby. *Tab+Enter* will publish the post.

4. Typing *q* moves you up or down to the **Chat** entry area. More about how chats work (quite well, thank you) later on.

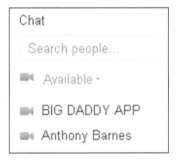

Sending a private message

If you want to use all the power of posts, including photos, videos, links, but want the message to go to just one person, that's easy.

I did it using another shortcut. Type a + or a @ and follow that (no leading space) with a part of their name, and you'll get a list of people, as shown in the following screenshot. Click on the one you want. In this case, I want to post to my lovely wife.

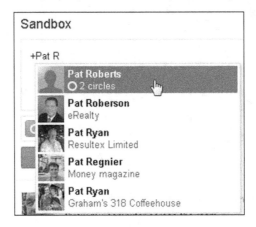

As I mentioned Pat in the post, she automatically gets a copy. Because I did not add any circles (a little **x** in the blue box lets you close any that might be open), only she gets the post (in her **Stream**).

Or, of course, you can use the new feature I gave you the tip on earlier and send an e-mail directly to that person. Again, click on their name to bring up their profile, then on the e-mail link just under their profile photo.

Below is what I send, a nice video I shot recently of a rainbow. You can watch it on my YouTube channel, http://youtube.com/ralphwroberts.

There are all sorts of permutations (combinations) of messages you can send. For example, you might send one that goes out to all the members of a club you belong to, but also add several friends, not members of the club, who might also be interested in the subject of the post.

Let me state again—there's a lot of power already in Google Plus, but it is still in the early days of its development. Expect the features I'm now showing you to continually be improved and new features added.

It's wonderful.

Editing your posts

Here's another neat feature on Plus—unlike Facebook, we can also edit our comments after posting! So, if you look at a comment you've posted on someone else's post (or even one of your own) and see a typo or decide to add something more, just click on the **Edit** link (looks like the following screenshot and is visible only to you).

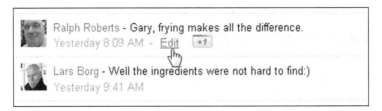

Make your changes and click on the **Save changes** button. The **Delete** comment button lets you remove the comment entirely and **Cancel** backs us out of editing mode without any changes being recorded.

Now, time to run around in circles, but you'll really enjoy it.

What's not to like about pluses?

Those of us who are also on Facebook understand Google's little **+1** symbol like in the following post. Yes, it's a way to like a post by letting others know about it. This is a notable difference to Facebook, as you'll see the little **+1** all over the Internet.

In the following example, I got distracted while writing when I came across Jason's post. He linked to an article that I'm interested in. I read it, and thanked Jason by giving him a plus. Be kind to those whose posts you like by awarding them +1s (just click on the small +1 icon under the post).

The basics of Circles

Circles give us the ability to organize all our contacts into groups. So, instead of having 836 friends, you have incredibly more manageable groups such as the ones Plus starts you with—*Friends*, *Acquaintances*, *Family*, and *Following* (people whose posts you wish to follow but not interact with, like on Twitter).

The above, as already touted more than once in this book and a lot more by Google+ folks and in reviews, is Google's stroke of genius. Circles is the killer feature setting Plus apart from other social media networks. Here are a couple of my circles:

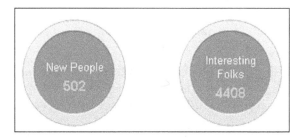

Like everyone else right now, I'm in the process of coming to terms with how circles work. I see all the advantages but, as many of us, have some bad, old Facebook habits to break.

On Facebook, the trap is the whole concept of friends. We're all in a competition to see how many hundreds of people we can friend. So, like many Facebookers, I have no clue who the heck the vast majority of these guys and gals are. I see someone with 172 mutual friends I invite them. It's a numbers game.

My Facebook account (http://facebook.com/rapidralph) has hundreds of folks clogging up my wall with constant posts and I often miss stuff my real friends post. Things I'd enjoy congratulating on, commiserating with, or just plain good-naturedly ragging them about. You know, the whole reason we're attracted to social networking in the first place.

In short, there's no control at all.

Plus gives us lots of control! To begin with, on the main or home page of Plus (your entry page after logging in), clicking on **Friends** shows only posts from the folks in your friends circle as I see in mine:

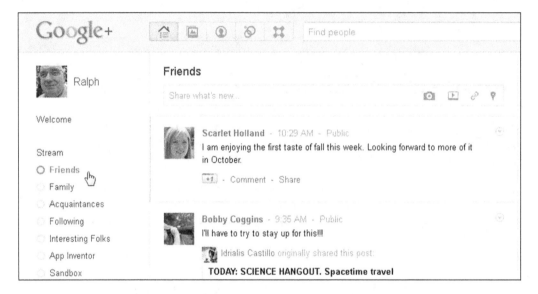

Click on **Stream** and all posts in any circle and those that are public from your circle-people show up. If you don't have anyone in your circles yet, then don't worry, later in this chapter I will show you how to connect with lots of people quickly.

Google wants you to have lots of folks in your circles. Social networking is only fun and attractive if you can interact with other people. So, they make that part (getting connections) really easy.

Who's following whom?

I mentioned Twitter earlier. Twitter works by allowing people to post short (140 character) messages. There is less interaction than on Facebook and now Plus because these twits, as they are called (posting a twit is called tweeting) do not have an easy provision for responding with comments. And, of course, with Plus we can have thousands of characters instead of just 140.

So on Twitter, you have *followers*—people who subscribe to your twits, tweets, whatever.

If you put out interesting things on Twitter (follow me on `http://twitter.com/ralphr` and Packt at `http://twitter.com/packtpub`) you get lots of followers, and you follow some fascinating folks. Yes, you can send messages or join Twitter groups, but the interaction is not on the same level as, say Facebook.

On Facebook, when you friend someone and they accept, your posts appear in their newsfeed and theirs in yours. It's much like being married to 900 people at one time. And that can be a problem, you're deluged with posts and—while there's plenty of scope for interaction—it's often hard to determine who is doing what, when.

You tend to miss (I do) interesting posts from real friends that you want to comment on.

We've emphasized several times already Google's addition of circles so that you can control that never-ending stream of posts, and drill down into the different rivulets and even essentially drop-by-drop. That's real power and we'll examine it in detail shortly.

However, in addition to Circles, Plus also gives you the Twitter-like power of controlling who you follow.

If someone friends you on Facebook, you either accept, getting all of his or her posts from now on and they get all of yours, or reject and both of you get nothing. On Twitter, just because 400 people are following you (seeing all your tweety twits) does not mean you have to follow them in return, and vice versa. If you're using social media to promote yourself or a product, then this can be good.

Take William Shatner.

Hey, I like William Shatner—Captain James T. Kirk of the original *Star Trek*. He's had by far the best career in comparison to anyone else from the original cast, and still has. A fascinating guy and I'm proud he's in my **Friends** circle on Plus:

How do I know this is really William Shatner? Or Sergey Brin and Larry Page (founders of Google? Or Mark Zuckerberg, the founder of competitor Facebook? Mark, ironically, has almost 500,000 people on Plus including him in their Circles—the most of anyone.

Now, while it may be pleasing to add celebrities, how do we know these people are real? Google recognizes that names can be easy to spoof (fake) on the Internet and has just added a new feature called **verification badges**. These badges indicate that the identity of celebrities, public figures, and just plain people who've been added to lots of Circles has been verified as legitimate identities by Google.

Click on the name of a celebrity in a post or in your Circles and this will bring up his or her profile page. Next to their name—if they are verified (remember, this is a huge task and it may be some time before everyone is vetted) will be a small gray circle with a blue checkmark in it. Run your cursor over the verification badge (as in Mr. Shatner's profile below) and the words **verified name** appear. This is a recently-added feature, but an important one.

Zuckerberg, by the way, may or may not be authentic. He has not been verified and—while he has near half a million who added him, he has absolutely no one in his Circles. Sounds like a bit of a prank to me.

Okay, so Captain Kirk has beamed into my Circles. Does this mean William Shatner reads all my posts and anxiously awaits my next? Nope. So far, Shatner has about 40,000 people who've included him in their Circles (you can get this info about anyone by looking at their profile). He has generously added about ten percent of those to his Circles, but for most of us, we see his posts but he does not see ours.

The above emphasizes the point that you do have control over posts appearing in your stream. Just because someone adds you does not mean (unlike Facebook) you have to add them.

On the other hand, putting people in your Circles is one way of getting them to add you.

It depends on your goals for Google Plus. A somewhat simplistic view shows us there are two types of Plus users:

1. **Followers**: Those who desire a limited profile on Plus, who want to interact with a few friends, colleagues, former schoolmates, fellow hobbyists, and so on, and perhaps follow some interesting celebrities by just reading their posts.

2. **Promoters**: Those who want to enhance their careers, espouse a cause, help their businesses, and so forth.

The truth is most of us are a combination of these basic types. And that's the wonderful thing about Plus. With all the varying degrees of control Circles afford us, we mix and match into any of the thousands of varying combinations. We could choose whatever suits us at the moment, and change that as circumstances require.

Now, how do we add people to our Circles?

Adding people to your Circles

My wife, Pat, kindly allows us to view her new Plus account so we can see setting up from the beginning and adding people to our Circles.

When we first access our new Plus account, we have no one in our Circles. Google knows this would quickly become quite boring, so they make it easy to find and add people.

To start out, there are a few suggestions from contacts in your Gmail account (also, Hotmail and Yahoo! accounts). You can put them in your Circles, but most of them will probably not be on Plus yet. As you add members of Plus, the system generates suggestions of other members you may want to add based on who you've already added.

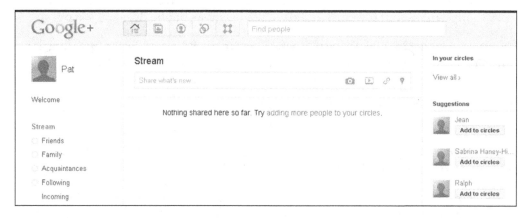

This brings us to the first way of attracting people we really want into our Circles — inviting them. Just click on **Send invitations** on the lower-right of your main page and an invitation dialog box appears. There's also a link you are encouraged to post in Internet groups or e-mail lists you frequent.

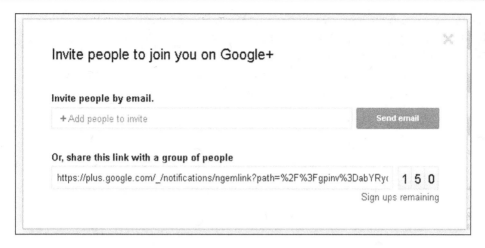

Most people—those you invite through direct e-mails or via groups—may take a while to respond. First, people have to figure out what Plus is, and then respond to the growing buzz and decide they want to be in on it. This can take days or even weeks.

Meanwhile, here are two faster ways of discovering folks and adding them.

Look at the center column of your main Plus page (following screenshot). The first method is to type the name of people who you think might be on Plus in the **Find people** box. Check for your friends, and so on.

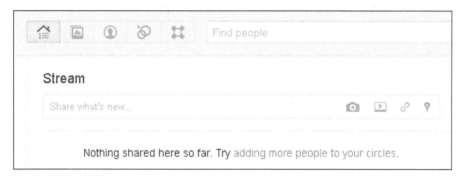

Want to add them wholesale? After you have added two, or three, or four people, especially those with a lot of connections, click on **add people to your circles** in order to add more, as shown in the preceding screenshot or click any time on **Show all** in the **Suggestions** area always on the right of your main Plus page.

Pat's first question on her new account was *"who are all these people?"* As she had added me, the system suggested not only contacts through her Gmail account, but all of my circle members!

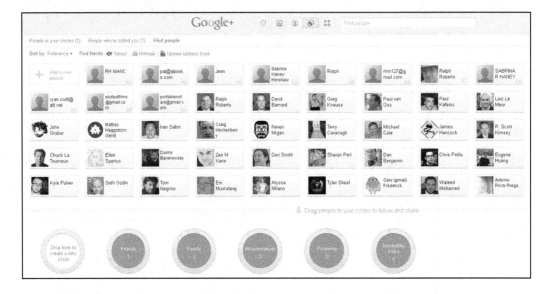

As you add Plus members, suggestions of those that can be added to your Circles grows exponentially (meaning in bunches). You could just add all these suggestions in your **Friends** circle, but that would just be recreating the Facebook problem all over again (a huge mass of people, you have no idea who they are, streaming posts you have no control over). So let's go for the best of both social networks, get a lot of contacts, but maintain control.

Now, I know many people starting out on any social network want to just add a few friends and be done with it. However, sooner or later (and this book shows you many reasons why "sooner" is better) you'll want to add lots more people.

Social networks—by their very definition—are all about social interaction. The more people you have connections with, the better are the things that can happen.

The problem (again for those of us from Facebook) is not getting connections, but managing them effectively. Otherwise, the incessant chatter can cause you to miss the good stuff you added all those people for in the first place.

We'll discuss creating customized Circles in greater detail later in this chapter but, for now, let's create a new circle enabling us to control interaction with all the new people we'll be adding. Click on **Show all** again. At the bottom of that screen are your existing Circles, which look like the following screenshot in a new account.

Click on **Create circle**.

A dialog box pops up. Enter Interesting Folks as the name of the new circle. Click on **Create empty circle** to create the new circle and save it (as shown):

We now have (at the right-end below), a new circle:

The purpose of the circle is to be a catchall, but we don't want to call it that, of course. No one can get insulted for being in your **Interesting Folks** circle. In the meantime, you can click on the circle and read their posts in your stream. If you don't like what they're posting, just delete them.

As far as finding out which Circles you're in, there is no good way currently. However, a new feature has been recently implemented allowing the sharing of Circles. So you can at least check and see if you're being recommended by others.

In the meantime, people will be adding you to their Circles and your posts will be getting a wider audience.

I mentioned the word *wholesale* in adding people to your Circles. Let's see how that works.

The following are the suggestions the Plus system is making in Pat's account. Hold down the *Shift* key and individually click on a lot of names (system lets you select all you want, but only one click at a time). Keeping the *Shift* key depressed, drag the selections down to the **Interesting Folks** circle.

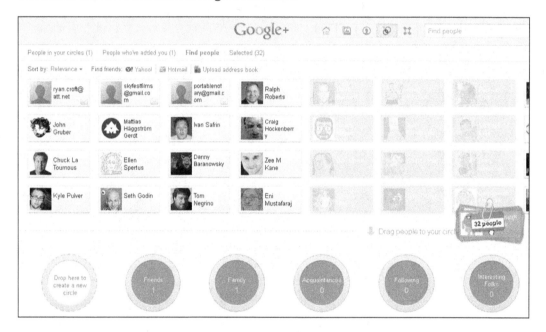

Now the **Interesting Folks** circle shows members:

And going back to the main page, we find a stream of posts from all these people. Your Plus account is coming to life!

Add even more at one time! At the top-right corner of the suggestions page, click on **More actions**, and then click on **Select all**.

Hold down the left mouse button, pull all the selections down slightly, wait a moment, and they all condense down, as shown in the following screenshot. Drop them on your **Interesting Folks** circle and they are all added!

Refresh the page and you'll get another 100 suggestions that you may also add. The system will let you do this a few times, then not give you any more suggestions for a while, but it's a good jump start if you want a lot of connections quickly. I've made more connections in three minutes than in two years on Facebook.

One more way to add is if you see an interesting commenter in a post. Just run move the cursor over his or her. A box pops up with information about them and a button, so that, if you like, they can be added to your Circles.

The more people added to your Circles, the more **notifications** you get.

Notifications

Notifications are messages from the system to you. Whenever someone adds you to their Circles (only to be expected if you're adding a bunch of people to yours) an automatic message is sent to you.

The little red box at the upper-right of the Google black **navbar** (navigation bar), shows the number of notifications. If the box is gray, you have no notifications. Click on the box to see notifications, as shown here:

If you have e-mail notifications turned on, messages about events also appear in your Gmail as seen in the following screenshot. These events include people adding you to their Circles and comments on your posts or those you've commented on.

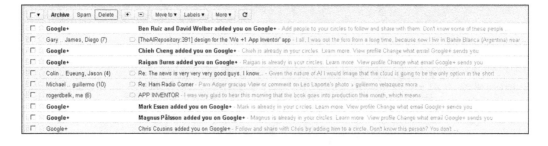

If you have the free Plus app for your phone, then you'll get notifications there as well, as on mine in the following image. This makes keeping up really convenient no matter where we might be.

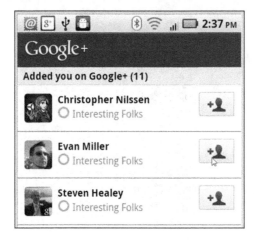

Creating new Circles

We saw how to create a circle above when we make our catchall Interesting Folks circle. You'll want to add other Circles based on your interests. The following are the ones I have so far, but I'll be creating others and pulling people out of Interesting Folks and sorting them in appropriate Circles.

The best strategy here is not to add too many. One of the features requested by many for Plus is the ability to add subcategories. That seems desirable and I expect we will get it pretty soon.

With these **subcircles**, you could have a main one called `School` and inside would be `Elementary`, `Junior High`, `High School`, and `College`.

However, it's your Plus account. Add as many or as few as you like because they can always be changed around later as often as needed.

Circles for Friends, Acquaintances, and Family

Plus starts you off with Circles for Friends, Acquaintances, and Family – those being pretty obvious and easy to fill assuming you can get your Uncle Ferd and Aunt Rose to join Plus.

Of course, it does not all have to be done at once. Add them as they decide to join you on Plus, but it's a great way to keep in touch will your friends, relatives, and acquaintances. All of these groups in separate Circles allow interaction to be appropriate to each.

Mastering circle maintenance

Maintaining Circles (moving, adding, deleting people) is simple. Click on the **Circles** logo as shown in the following screenshots and you'll have access to everyone in all your Circles. I'm up to 1288 people now, which means I have a lot of sorting out to do.

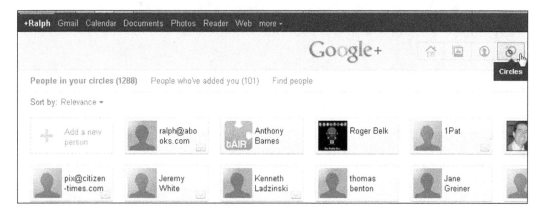

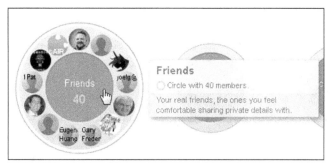

To drill down to just one circle, such as my **Friends** circle below, click on the name of the circle (in its blue circle at the bottom of the page), and we get a pop-up dialog box as follows:

While the preceding procedure is okay for quick operations, such as adding a new person, it is more of a launch pad than an end point for circle maintenance. Let's look at the bottom line of the box:

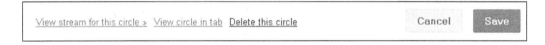

Over to the right is the **Cancel** button (stops the operation, closes the box) and **Save** (saves your changes such as the new friend added, and so on).

Now back to the three links on the bottom left:

1. View Stream for this circle: Lets us see only those posts from people in this circle.

2. View circle in tab: Very useful view for maintenance. Closes the dialog box and spreads everything for the selected circle out as shown in the following screenshot.

3. Delete this circle: Be careful, this choice will delete the entire circle and all people in it who are not in any of your other Circles. The system gives you one chance (a user-friendly message) to abort.

We now have our circle (following screenshot) in a nicely viewable page. Let's see what we can do to it.

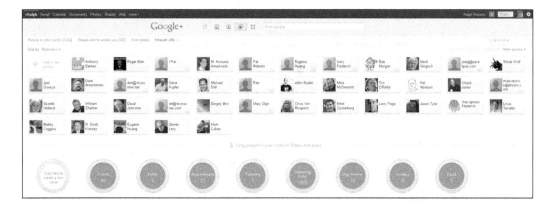

First, we can select people by simply clicking on them and they stay selected (that is, we can have multiple selections).

Look at the upper-right corner of the page (following screenshot). In the **Type a name** box, we can search for names. Not too useful in this circle with only 40 members, all of whom can be seen on the screen as is true above, but if we go to my Interesting Folks circle with over 1200 already, a search feature is obviously very handy.

The following line would let us remove the selected people, clear the selection (deselect them), view their profile (only works on a single selection, grayed out for multiple), and gives us a drop-down menu called **More actions**.

The **More actions** drop-down menu (following screenshot) we've already seen. We used it earlier to select everyone on the screen showing suggested connections for us to add them en masse, a hundred at a time.

This menu also allows you to block people whose posts you don't want to see but want to keep in the circle. Furthermore, you can check to see who you have blocked by clicking on **View blocked**.

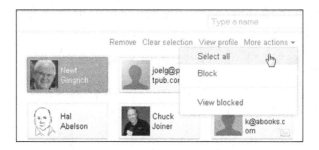

Sorting Circles

One of the major things we'll be doing a lot is sorting people into various Circles. I've selected (single click) James Rhodes as an example. James works for Zipline Games. I can view his profile by double-clicking. In the past, I've written books about games and might again. So, it could be good to have a **Games** circle.

Once my Games circle is created, I just drag-and-drop James into it, as shown in the following screenshot. Now, I have the choice of leaving him in Interesting Folks (dragging does not delete) or deleting him (use **Remove** as we saw in the preceding section).

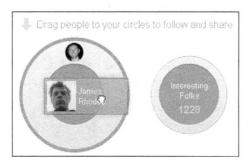

Say, having a Games circle (or whatever specific category you want for your own circle) is a good idea. Let's search those 1228 names in Interesting Folks and see how many are connected with games. ... Shucks, it only finds ones with Games in the name. Well, that's a start. I can select those and move them, but looks like the profiles are not being searched.

Must be a better way? Actually, there is. In the `Find people` search box at the top of most Plus screens, type the topic you want in the `Find people` box. In this case, that would be `games`. (This has now changed to 'Search Google+' and is available on all screens at the top.)

Google's search links me in 13 seconds to over four million profiles related to games.

Clicking on the top profile returned gives me Christer Kaitila's Plus profile. Oh, he's already in my Interesting Folks. Just have to search for him there and drop him into Games.

Of course four million is a bit unwieldy, the search term needs refinement. Putting in `game developer` (more like what I would be looking for) brings it down to 783,000, and `computer game developer` gives a mere 212,000.

Craft your search terms well and you can drill way down to get the types of people you'd love to have in a specific kind of circle.

Adding people who've added you

We definitely want to add those who add us first! Click on the **Circles** tab (top of the screen), then on **People who've added you**. Click on **Sort by:** and choose **Not yet in circles**.

Run your cursor over the ones at the top. If you see **In no circles**, look at their profile and decide which circle they belong in. Drag-and-drop them there.

Reordering Circles

Once you get several rows of Circles you'll probably want to reorder them from time to time. Just move the cursor onto the one to be moved, hold down the left mouse button, drag the circle to its new position, and release the button.

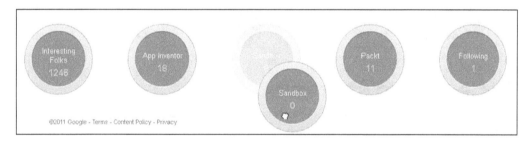

Sorting members of a circle

In the preceding section, we mentioned sorting in finding people who have added you, but you have not yet added to your Circles. Other kinds of sorting may be accomplished in each of your Circles.

Referring to the following figure, you can sort by first name, last name, relevance (where Plus tries to guess what kind of people you like, not really useful until you have a lot), and by ones who have recently updated, that is, posted.

Circle editing shortcuts

By right-clicking on any circle (as shown in the following screenshot), you open a menu that allows four choices. The first is used to edit the circle's description and gives links to other functions. We saw this screen already—it's the dialog box that popped up and we used the link at the bottom to get into the tab view (all the people spread out for ease of editing).

The second, **View circle in tab**, saves us one step in getting that spread out view. The third lets us view all the posts of people in that circle, and the third deletes the entire circle. Just shortcuts, but it's always good to know there are several ways of accomplishing the same tasks.

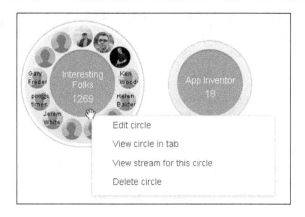

Private Circles

It's possible to make Circles private, if you wish. If you put someone in a private circle, then no one can tell you're following that person. Otherwise, you show up in his or her profile.

To make a circle private, click on **Profile** in the top menu bar, then on **Change who is visible here** (following screenshot) in the lower-left of the profile page.

A dialog box like this one comes up. Click on **All circles**.

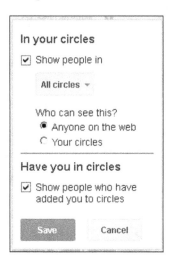

Another menu appears. Uncheck whichever Circles you wish to be private (they can be made public again any time you like). In my case, **Sandbox** is used for testing so I've made it private. The rest I want people to see.

Following celebrities and others

Quite a few celebrities have already adopted Plus. You'll run across them. If you want to add them faster, then check out http://www.recommendedusers.com/. There are various categories (a few shown in the following screenshot) of celebrities with links to profiles, making it easy for you to add them.

What we learned

In this chapter, we explored in detail the basics of using Plus! We learned how Circles work and their tremendous advantages and set up our first Circles.

We also saw how to decide who we want to follow and found out how to do so. We mastered easy dragging and dropping in maintaining our circles.

We created and used new types of Circles beyond the standard ones and were introduced to various tips and shortcuts making all of the above the joy it should be.

Now — let's get visual and go all video on our friends and other folks on Plus.

3
Hanging Out

Other social media systems are adding video chat and related features. Plus was designed from the ground up with these fun and powerful things built in!

In this chapter, we will see (literally see) how **Hangout**s work. We will explore:

- What Hangouts are and how we use them
- Setting up a webcam or other video input
- Creating your own Hangouts
- Joining existing Hangouts
- Hanging Out from YouTube

Here I am in an enjoyable hangout a few nights ago (me on the far right). As we'll see again, several times in this chapter, there is a row at the bottom of every Hangout session showing everyone in the video chat who has their camera on (not everyone does, in fact you can use just a microphone).

The person speaking will be shown in a larger video just above this row, but more of that shortly.

First, let's discuss exactly what a Hangout is in Google Plus.

What Are Hangouts?

A Hangout is a video conference where you and up to 5,000 (somewhere close to the current limit of chatters in one Hangout) of your closest friends (or absolute strangers) gather. Google stresses, in the Plus introductory material (following screenshot) to hangouts, the casual aspect—you and your buddies wandering in and out to chat.

However, in these early days in Google where everyone is kind of still feeling their way around, video chats seem to be a bit more structured. There are not many of them yet and they are hard to find as Plus does not show a comprehensive list of which are active.

Entering a search for the word hangout in the search box at the top of the main Plus page does not yield any useful information. Luckily, there is a third party site—that finds and lists both scheduled hangouts and those active (as shown in the following screenshot). Active hangouts have a blue button named **Join this hangout**. Left-click on it to join.

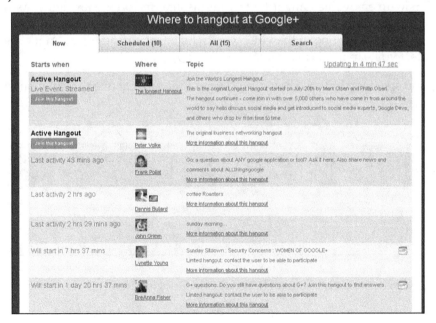

In the introductory tour to the concept of Hangouts, Google tells us (in the following screenshot) that *"the unplanned meet-up comes to the web for the first time."* And, indeed, if someone starts a hangout, they can specify which circles it appears in.

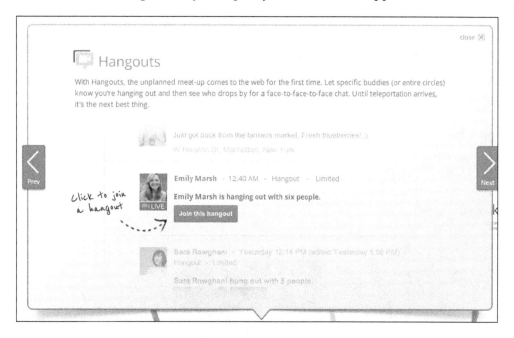

The Plus site offers this information about how one gets in a Hangout:

- If you start a **Hangout**, a post will appear in their stream telling them that there's a hangout going on, along with all the people in that hangout currently.

- If 25 or fewer people are invited, then they'll receive a notification that they've been invited to join a hangout.

- If you invite individuals that are signed in to Plus, then they'll receive an IM with a link to join.

- If someone invited to a hangout tries to start their own, then they'll be told that there's a hangout already going on and they may want to join that one instead.

- As the hangout you're in is visible by the circles of the other hangout participants, people you don't know may learn that you're hanging out and join. This is all very much like a conventional video conference.

Of course, you can click on Hangouts for real time info on open hangouts.

If you start a hangout in your Friends circle, then only your friends will see it and, thus, only they can enter. Tagging it `Public` lets anyone enter.

To start a Hangout, click on **Start a hangout** (below, bottom of right column, main Plus page).

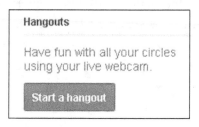

In the following example (after making sure my camera and microphone are working), I choose **Friends** so that only the 44 friends in my circle can join. In a little while, I'll show you how to wake them up and let them know you're online.

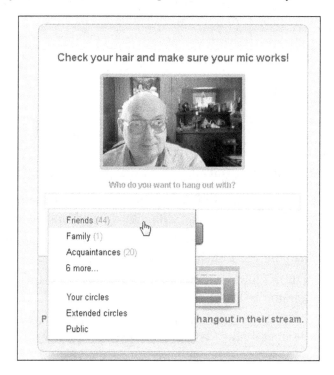

Why would you want to hang out in a video chat?

Here are some reasons:

1. Conversations are even more enjoyable when we can see what everyone is doing while the person speaking (like my friend Edward Robinson here). Visuals make chat yet more realistic. Just like a meeting of friends in our living rooms, but this one can be literally spread worldwide.

2. It's the easiest way of interacting on the computer. Just sit back in a comfortable chair, like Edward above, and talk. Once you're in the chat, you don't have to touch the keyboard. Just talk when you feel like it or someone asks you a question.

3. It's the most human way of using a computer because people like to talk. You might tell me you don't, but you tell me. I know you want to say more, now you can.

4. It's easy to hold things up and display these objects to make a point. Discussing your cellphone? Hold it up close to the camera so everyone can see.

Of course, using video like hangouts calls need a camera and a microphone (or at least a microphone). Bet that's downright expensive, eh? Nope. Let's select and set up our camera next.

Selecting and setting up a webcam

Chatting on the web in general and in hangouts specifically requires a video camera (for picture) and a microphone to pick up the sound of your voice.

A **webcam** is a USB device (plugs into the USB port on your computer) with a camera and a built-in microphone designed specifically for video conferencing. Webcams are inexpensive and readily available just about everywhere these days. In your local big box electronic goodies store, office supply stores, Walmart, everywhere.

Or you can do like I did after finding out the old webcam lying around did not supply the quality of picture or sound desired — pop over to eBay on the web and search for *webcam*. I found the one below for $5.99 plus $1 shipping. Sure, it was in Hong Kong, but arrived here in North Carolina in little over a week, and works perfectly for hangouts.

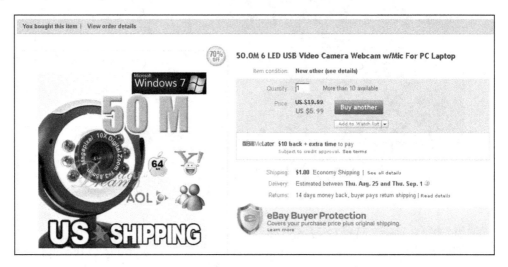

Most inexpensive webcams these days require little more than plugging them into a USB port. They install themselves ("plug and play" technology). If additional support is needed for installation, such as drivers, then a disk is included.

To see if your webcam works on Plus, click on the green **Start a hangout** button in the lower part of the right column of the main Plus page. If you can see yourself, then the camera part of your webcam is working. If not, then troubleshoot the problem before proceeding by making sure your webcam is working properly on your computer.

Talk and look at the little microphone at the bottom of this figure. If green bars go up and down when you speak, then it works.

Furthermore, something new here! We can now see live hangouts listed that we can join.

We're now ready to start our own hangout, or to join those already in progress.

Starting your own Hangout

By now, we've already seen that pressing the green **Start a hangout** button does just that.

So, let's start up a Hangout and play with the controls in order to learn what they do. We'll do this in a circle where you have few or no members. And we'll open it with nothing selected to make sure it is completely private for testing purposes.

First, here are three more points from the Google Plus site about who can invite others or join hangouts:

1. Hangouts are created by one person, but everyone in the hangout shares the ability to invite others.

2. Each hangout has a specific URL. That URL can be shared as a link to invite others. However, only Google+ users are able to join.

3. Be thoughtful when inviting as you can't kick anyone out of a hangout. If you feel uncomfortable in a hangout you can leave at any time.

And a warning about your e-mail address!

When you appear in someone's chat list in Google+, it's possible that person could discover your e-mail address. While your e-mail address won't be displayed in the chat list in Google+, it is displayed in the chat lists of other Google products (Gmail and iGoogle, for instance). The members of chat lists are consistent across Google products.

That said, you're pretty safe in hangouts—let's see how they work. Go ahead and start your Hangout so you can follow along and test out these things. Remember to start this in a little used or private circle (best) so that people won't be popping in while you're learning.

First, you should notice the thumbnail video player showing the input from your webcam. Look at the line of icons below your image (or mine in the following screenshot). These are the controls you use while in hangouts.

Beginning from left to right:

- **Invite**: This control allows us to invite additional people into our chat. This works in two ways. You can start typing a name, as follows, and let the system find it for you:

You can invite entire circles or make the chat public using this same dialog box. Clicking on the **Share** icon again causes these pop up boxes to disappear.

- **Chat**: The next control over adds a text chat to the hangout where you can type messages as follows:

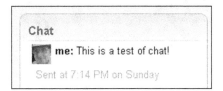

And even use **emoticons** (funny icons) as follows. Click on **Chat** again to collapse it out of sight.

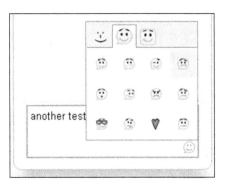

While this may seem to contradict the ease I mentioned earlier of just sitting back and talking, it's still a useful adjunct to have.

- **YouTube**: Allows us to actually search for, find, and show videos on YouTube to the group in our hangout, and even to talk over video using the **Push to talk** button as we follow:

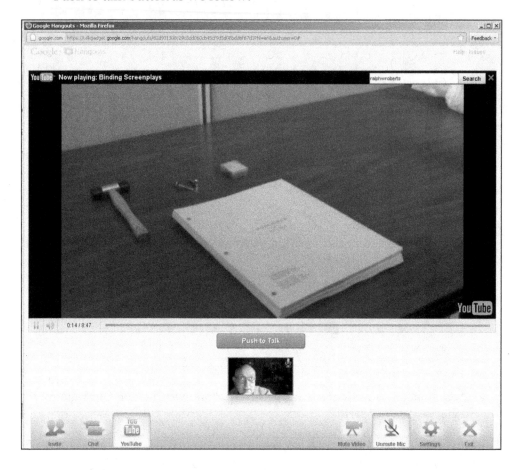

Note that the microphone is muted while the video plays, hence the need for the push to talk feature.

- **Mute Video**: Moving over to the right, clicking on the Mute Video control causes your image to go black. If you want to scratch or something, then hide the video temporarily.

- **Mute Mike**: Need to blow your nose? Use both the **Mute Video** and **Mute Mic** buttons. Please.

- **Settings**: Allows us to change settings related to our camera. If you're not getting picture or sound, then come here to check settings. Click on **Save** or **Cancel changes** to exit.

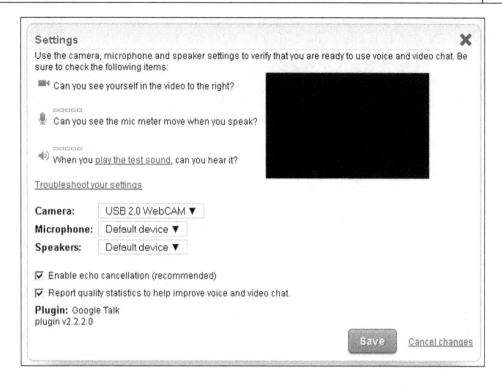

- **Exit**: This button takes you out of the hangout. If others are still in it, the hangout continues, otherwise it closes.

Now you are ready to start your own hangouts with the individuals or various members of circles you invited. Have fun!

Joining existing Hangouts

Here's what happens when you look for and join an existing hangout. You could start with the one at the top of this web page, billed as the world's longest hangout, it's been running since July 20th, 2011.

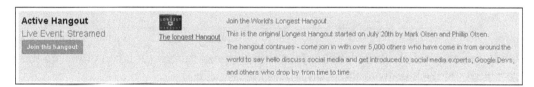

In my case (and for this example) I looked for a smaller hangout and found one hosted by Frank Poliat, a nice guy with several helpful folks in the hangout.

Checking Frank's hangout post before joining the chat, I saw only one other person was in there—looked like a good place to start (and it was).

Ready to enter, I clicked on the blue **Join this hangout** button (you can either do this from the post itself or from the gphangout.com website).

A dialog box, such as the one shown in the following screenshot, comes up and I can see all the members of the hangout before committing to join it. So I click to hang out. And, yeah, it does not take me long to check my hair.

Inside the hangout (a new browser window is opened), Frank is speaking, so he is in the large video. The three members of this hangout (myself included now) are shown below. These are all live video shots so you can watch the actions and reactions of everyone.

Moving the cursor over any of the small videos at the bottom shows a microphone control (it lets us mute an individual), the red hand lets us report someone abusive, and if we click on the person's name, then his profile shows in your original browser.

You can read the profile and perform any other action you like in the first instance of your browser while the video chat continues in the second.

If you spend too much time just watching instead of occasionally participating (talking), then the system will want to know if you're still awake. Click on **Yes** to stay in the hangout.

If a video thumbnail is black, then it means that the participant has the video turned off, or is not using a camera, as shown in the following screenshot:

When you exit the hangout you are reminded to close this instance of your browser, as follows:

This is what people see in the posts on their stream when you are in a hangout (that's me, in the middle). However, for a while we had several more people in the chat.

So that was my first real hangout and I was in it for over an hour. I really enjoyed myself and made several new friends that I've hung out with since. Jump in and you'll enjoy it too.

Hanging out from YouTube

Google owns YouTube so their latest feature for Plus—allowing us to start hangouts from YouTube—was easy for them to implement.

The following is one of my trip videos driving through the North Carolina mountains (see my YouTube channel). Note at the bottom-right of the following screenshot the link now appearing on YouTube videos when **Share** is clicked—**Start a Google+ Hangout**.

Clicking on the preceding link on the YouTube page causes Plus to open our now familiar start-a-hangout dialog box. We choose what groups we wish to share the showing and discussion of this video with (that is, who can join the chat). We then click on **Hang out**.

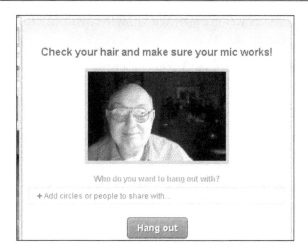

The hangout then opens with your chosen video playing. The video may be one of your own or any other on YouTube on which you want to get a discussion going.

Note that the YouTube button in the controls at the bottom below is automatically depressed and the microphone muted. When others join the hangout, they and you use the **Push to talk** button to make comments over the video's audio track.

To stop the video—such as while you are waiting for people to join your hangout—click on the **YouTube** control.

When enough people have joined and you want to start the video, click again on the **YouTube** button and the video starts replaying from the beginning.

It's a very neat and powerful feature, yes?

This completes the chapter on the Hangout video conferencing abilities of Plus. Go forth and see what you can, yes, see.

What we learned

So we now know what Hangouts are and how we use them. We saw how easy setting up a webcam or other video input is, and how to create our own Hangouts.

We also found two ways of finding and joining existing Hangouts. The first being notifications in our streams and the second being the new feature on that *check your hair* dialog, showing us active hangouts right in Plus, as follows:

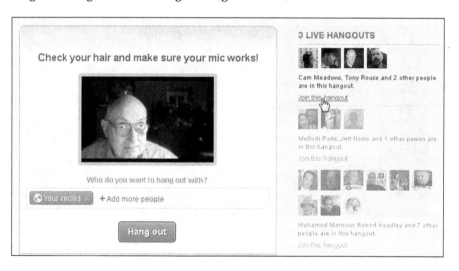

And finally, we learned to initiate a new hangout with associated video in the sharing feature of YouTube.

Next, we look at streams.

4
Streaming

Streams are somewhat like the News Feed in Facebook, except in Plus you control where your posts appear.

For example, you might wish your brother a happy birthday in your `Family` circle and kid a buddy in your `Bowling League` circle about the gutter shot he rolled last night. In your `Work` circle, you post something work-related and so on and so on.

So in this chapter we will:

- See how **Stream** works, practice posting, and determine how to drill down so that each post goes to the right audience.
- Learn how to control what we see and when we see it (as opposed to all those zillions of posts you're not interested in, but which make you miss the good stuff on other social networks).

In the following illustration is an example of how articles you post may be shared by others.

I like posting interesting articles about space (longtime space enthusiast, worked with NASA, and so on) and seek out such articles on the web to post on Plus.

Posts on Plus may be a few words or a few hundred. You can have no photos, one photo, or literally scores of photos. It's quite flexible and we'll be seeing the different ways you can use this powerful feature.

Here's an example. In Streams, another person picked up the following post by me, thus sending it out to people not in my circles, which results in more people adding me to their circles.

This is an ideal situation, something we'll discuss more here and also in *Chapter 7, Google+ on Your Mobile Device*, about how to promote yourself, your business, or a product on Plus.

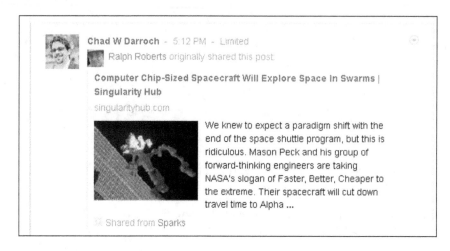

First, everything changes, especially social networks in beta testing phase.

Changelog

The thing about writing computer books when a project is still in early testing is it changes! In my opinion, however, that's the only time to write about computer (and other web-related) topics,otherwise your book is too late to do any good.

Anyway, I like to keep my readers up-to-date, hence the inclusion of brief **changelogs** (quick intros of significant new features) occasionally.

In the past few days, Google has added two new features to Plus—the way notifications of people adding you to their circles is shown, and the `Ignore` feature (which limits what the ignored person can share with you).

First, when you get added to circles, it occurs in one of two ways. Someone sees your posts, thinks you are cool (well, we are), and adds you to one of their circles.

Or you've added someone whose contributions have caught your eye, and they return the favor by adding you. That's the basic way you gain followers on Plus.

Now (with this new feature) Plus breaks it down and shows which way you got added (and the more circles you're in, the more people see your posts).

As we see in the following screenshot (in a **Notification** to me), two new people have added me (I add them back, but make your own choice after checking their profiles by clicking on their names). Furthermore, eight folks already in my circles now have included me in theirs, no action necessary for that.

The second change might be termed a civility feature. Earlier we saw how to block people, but that seems a bit harsh. So, Plus now has an `Ignore` feature, as shown.

To get there, left-click on the small circles icon at the top of the main Plus page, which takes you to your circles maintenance page. Then, click on **People who've added you**, which lists all the kind folk who now have you in their circles.

Click on any individual and the `Ignore` feature becomes active.

Including the preceding, there are three places you can ignore people from:

1. The `notifications in your Google+` bar.
2. Your `Incoming` stream.
3. Under the `People who have added you` **tab while** `editing your circles`.

When we ignore a person:

- They'll be removed from the `People who have added you` list
- New content from them will no longer be delivered to your `Incoming` stream, and content they've already shared will be removed from `Incoming`
- Their `mentions` of you won't appear in your stream and you won't receive a notification from them

Anytime you'd like to see the list of all the people you've ignored, just go to the `People who have added you` list, click on `More actions` and select `View ignored`.

If you add an ignored person to one of your circles, then they are removed from the ignored list.

Ignoring someone is not the same as blocking. Ignored persons can still comment on your public posts, tag you in photos (that's coming up later in the book), and add you to their circles. You will still receive notifications when they tag you.

Furthermore, ignored persons may appear on those automatic suggestions from Plus of people you might want to add (adding an ignored person, of course, removes their ignored status).

If you want no interaction at all with someone, then block them instead of ignoring.

Now, let's look at the end product of sparks and posts which occur in the Stream.

How the Stream works

If you've been on Facebook, the Google Plus **Stream** works in a similar manner. People post updates (a few words or many about what's happening in your life or anything else)—which may include photos, videos, and web links.

The major difference here is we control which posts we want to see! In the following screen capture, I've selected **Stream**, which shows all my circles and all public posts (tell you about those in a moment). On the screen, the circle selected (**Stream** here) is shown in red.

Should I want to limit the posts streaming by, it's easy to select Friends or Family or any of my circles by left-clicking on the title. Currently, only one circle at a time may be selected in this manner. Again, Stream shows them all.

Controlling what we see

Taking a closer look at the list of circles above, we see **More** with a small downwards-pointing arrow. Clicking (tapping the left button on your mouse) causes the lists of circles to expand, revealing all circles as follows. Clicking on **Less** collapses them again to the compact list as shown in the preceding screenshot.

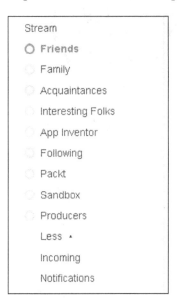

Clicking on **Incoming** (second from bottom above) displays posts shared with you by people who aren't in your circles. To share a post with a specific person, mention them by name in the post using a plus + symbol in front of their name such as +Ralph Roberts or +Dolly Parton (yes, she's on Plus and quite active).

Add people you want to follow and share with by clicking on their names and adding them to the circle or circles you want them to be in, as follows:

In `Incoming`, you can hide stuff you're not interested in by selecting **Mute this post**, as follows, (nah, I didn't really mute you, Tyler).

At the bottom of that group, we have **Notifications**. All notifications of people adding you to their circles are shown here. This is a good thing because the higher the number of people that add you, the higher the number of people that see your posts!

Remember `Extended Circles` from *Chapter 2, Joining Plus and What to Do First*? This is a truly powerful secret way of augmenting your read. By posting to `Your Circles` and adding `Extended Circles`, your posts go not just to your circles, but also to the folks in their circles. Say you have only twenty people following you, but one of those has 100,000. Yes, real power—you suddenly have a vast potential audience!

Here we see a list of those who've added you recently:

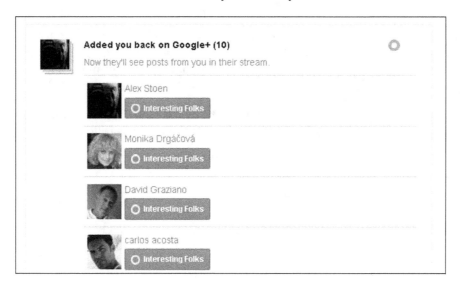

Clicking on the small circle at the top-right above (it's green on the screen) provides us with the choices shown in the following screenshot. In this way, you can keep track of people noticing you (hence, the overall title of Notifications).

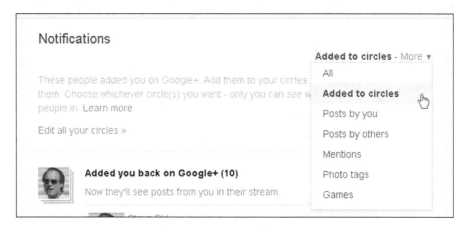

And, of course, you can get notifications in your Gmail account, by clicking the little red notification icon in the Google toolbar, or (if you have the Google+ app installed on your phone or tablet) while you're in the grocery store shopping or anywhere else you might be!

So far in discussing Streams, we've discovered that:

1. Clicking on **Streams** shows all current posts, updating in real time without the necessity of refreshing the page. If you have several hundred people you're following, then this is an almost constant process (hence why the name stream fits).

2. Selecting the name of a circle, such as **Friends** or **Family**, shows only posts from your friends or family. The name of the selected circle is in red.

3. The **More** and **Less** links expand or collapse your lists of circles respectively.

4. **Incoming** shows posts from people who have mentioned you in their posts and you can add them to your circles.

5. **Notifications** show who's adding you and who you've added.

Posting and Targeting

The two most frequent activities you'll be doing on Plus are reading and posting. It's a safe assumption that you already know how to read—if not, see me after class. Here's a quick review of how to post.

At the top of the middle portion of the main Plus screen, click in the **Share what's new...** box. This expands the box to several lines with four icons in the lower-right. Clicking on these icons allows us to add photos, videos, web links, and our geographic location.

As shown in the following screenshot, we post by typing in our post. Special characters allow emphasis—text between asterisks (*) bold, underscores (_) italicize, and a hyphen (-) strikes through.

Select additional circles to share with (or **Public**) by clicking on **+Add more people**. You can also add people not yet on Plus from your Gmail account.

The post, when the **Share** button is clicked to publish it, looks like this:

Why do we post and what do we post?

Good questions. Basically, you can post anything you feel like. "My dog just burped," is perhaps not of great interest, however.

In Plus, unlike Facebook, when you "friend" someone by placing them in one of your circles, it does not mean they automatically follow you as well. That is, you'll be seeing their posts but unless they make the effort of putting you into their circles, they will not be seeing yours.

Here's the secret of posting successfully on Plus:

 Post links to interesting and/or timely articles. Then, as people comment on them, answer the comments pushing your posts back up the stream and generating yet more interaction.

Let's look at my post about the Blythe Intaglios as an example. *Intalglio* is a fancy word to describe how huge drawings only seen easily from the sky, such as the famous Nazca Lines in Peru, were made—that is, carving an image into a surface, in this case the earth itself.

There are three ways in which people respond about our posts:

1. **+1**: Similar to Like on Facebook, giving a post a quick +1 shows the reader enjoyed, learned from it, was amused, or whatever. A brief spatter of applause, so to speak. In the preceding article, I've received seven +1s so far. Clicking on the number shows you who likes you, as follows:

2. **Share**: If someone really thinks your post is keen, they Share it by reposting to their groups. You can do the same by clicking on the **Share** link on other people's posts. In the case of this article, two kind folks have shared it (click on **Shares** on the screen to see who). This can be really good for you. (For example, here my friend Steven Vaughan-Nichols, a well-known computer writer with a much larger following than mine, shared my post.) It means a lot of people outside your circles see it and (if they like you) add you to their circles, and your footprint on Plus grow.

3. **Comment**: Third are comments, which occur when people are inspired enough by your post to write something about it, as follows:

The preceding screenshot consist of some of the comments on my post. Note that some of them are mine where, like in my tip above, I am interacting with commenters, which generates yet more interest.

Another suggestion: When reading public posts you like that have lots of +1s, shares, and comments, click on each of those three categories to show who those people are. If they like what you like, then they're great candidates to add to your own circles. Just click on their name and choose a circle of yours to put them in.

Targeting

Two concepts fall under the term **targeting**. Targeting simply means posting things that interest a particular group. Plus lends itself well in both ways we're now discussing.

First, if you choose a particular circle — such as Friends or Family or School — you pretty much know what interests them. The same goes for any of your other circles, so that's our easy concept.

A bit vaguer might be how to target groups when we're doing `Public` posts that many people may be reading.

The following is an example. I'm writing this book on Plus. The more people who know that, frankly, the more books we'll sell (and thanks again to you for buying it). So in this post, I shared an article about the controversial real name policy. In the two days since I posted, this shared article post has generated 97 comments posted to it.

A point we'll emphasize several times in this book: the more comments, shares, and +1s your posts generate, the greater the number of followers you'll gain. You get out of it what you put in! The last chapter of this book covers all the good stuff the right kind of promotion brings.

By the way I do not think it will be going away. Both Facebook and Google are competing for the identity market. That is, they want to be able to build products for commerce and other things that rely on verified identities.

Eric Schmidt, Chairman of Google, was quoted in a recent *Washington Post Business* article that the Internet would be better if people were identified by their true identities.

I don't see Google backing off the real name requirement at all. It means too much for them. As Schmidt is also reported saying, Google+ was built primarily as an identity service and that those worried about using their real names shouldn't use the service.

I'm convinced Plus is worth it.

Another type of promotional targeting is pushing products you might be selling more directly. While writing *"Google App Inventor by Example"*, *Packt Publishing*, I created a number of apps, including the following one, which I sell.

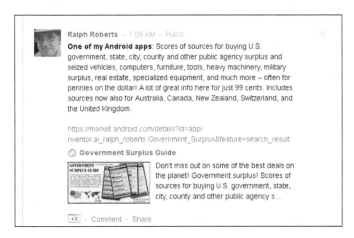

However, don't just blatantly run ads for yourself or your company all the time or people will ignore you. Entertain also. I have a talent for finding oddball, but interesting things on the Internet, such as the *Hanging Temple of Hengshan* article in the following post. Being interesting builds followers!

To tie up the two concepts of targeting above, think of who your audience is. Posting in your `Friends` circle is different than trying to reach a specific subset of a public post that thousands might be reading. Tailor your posts to the group reading them.

Posts are content, whether that content is something you write, writing by someone else, photos, videos, or just links to interesting stuff on the web. These posts come from two different sources—items you have on your own computer or content you link to on the web.

Let's look at your stuff first.

Posting your own stuff

Probably the first things of your own you'll want to post are photographs. In this age of smartphones with cameras, we all have lots of photos and the ability to generate more any time we like.

The next chapter in this book is about preparing and posting pictures, videos, and other media, but let's look at just the basics of posting here.

To start with, if you have a smartphone with the official Google+ app installed, Plus automatically uploads the photos from your phone. This can be disabled during installation of the Google Plus app now, by the way.

It's easy to post them. Start a post, as I have in the following screenshot, in my `Friends` circle, by clicking in the **Share What's New...** box. If photos have been uploaded, then you'll see that indicated as the leftmost icon at the bottom of the input textbox. The little **6** shows me I have six photographs from my phone.

Plus groups your phone's photos by dates (as shown in the following screenshot) and tags them with geographic locations if that option is turned on. Don't worry, we learn how to delete phone photos and turn off the location, if that's what you want, in the next chapter.

Clicking on the next icon to the right—the little camera (it's green on the screen)—opens a drop-down menu (which follows). In this menu, you can add photos (from your computer), create an album of several photos, or also add from your phone.

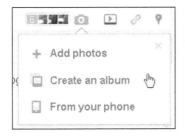

Clicking on **Add photos** opens directories on your local computer or network. Choose a photo to upload, caption, and publish on Plus in a matter of seconds (again, more details in the next chapter).

In the same manner, you may also upload videos from your computer using the **Upload video** choice on the drop-down menu from the small video icon (red arrow in a circle), or from your phone if you have the Google+ app installed.

Okay, more about photos and videos in *Posting from the web* seen later in this chapter and, of course, in *Chapter 5, Streaming and Sparking Up Some Interest*. First, let's consider how to post other types of files.

Posting Other types of documents

Plus does not yet allow us to just attach any kind of file, so we have to make minor conversions.

One kind of file we probably have in large quantities and might want to post from time to time are text files. These are probably in one of the three formats:

1. Plain text with hard returns at the end of lines.

2. Word processor files are in **WYSIWYG (What You See Is What You Get)** such as .doc files from Microsoft Word, and so on. These have soft returns for breaking lines inside a paragraph and hard returns at the end of paragraphs. Both text files and word processor files will require a bit of extra effort to post—we will show you that in a moment.

3. PDF (Adobe's Portable Document Format) files are nice because they retain all the formatting, graphics, fonts, and so on of the original PDF document. There are several PDF writing programs (some free) available to generate these files.

    ° **Converting Plain Text Files**: The hard line returns in both plain text and word processor files mess them up. You can't just cut and paste. In plain text, it's necessary to remove the hard returns inside paragraphs.

Here's an example. I found a humorous quote by Albert Einstein in my old e-mail perfect for a post. He's explaining how radio works (tongue firmly in cheek).

When I cut and pasted the quote into the Plus post textbox, it looked like this:

> *"You see, the telephone is a kind of a very, very long cat. You pull his*
> *tail in New York and his head is meowing in Los Angeles. Do you understand*
> *this? And the radio operates exactly the same way: you send signals*
> *here, they receive them there. The only difference is that there is no*
> *cat."*

Funny but difficult to read because those hard returns cause line breaks in the wrong places. You want a flexible line break that looks good on all those hundreds of kinds of screens your readers will be viewing? So simply delete at the end of lines that break wrong, and insert a space so that our quote now looks like this:

> *"You see, the telephone is a kind of a very, very long cat. You pull his tail in New*
> *York and his head is meowing in Los Angeles. Do you understand this? And the*
> *radio operates exactly the same way: you send signals here, they receive them there.*
> *The only difference is that there is no cat."*

That's it. Makes the text readable, and makes you look like you know what you're doing (which now you do!).

- **Converting word processor files**: In a word processor file, we have pretty much the opposite problem, in that, it's the soft returns causing the trouble. Here's how we fix that.

I came across a short story written years ago that I want to post. It's in Word and a standard manuscript format as the first paragraph, as follows:

```
      The Dog ignored the proceedings, some heads yawning, some

panting with tongues lolling under the hot television lights.

Five leash chains occasionally rattled as one head or the other

moved, or the body twitched. The Human was a different matter —

he twitched more.
```

Cutting and pasting into the post textbox gives the following result. See how some words run together now? That's where the soft returns were in the Word file.

Stream

The Dog ignored the proceedings, some heads yawning, somepanting with tongues lolling under the hot television lights. Five leash chainsoccasionally rattled as one head or the other moved, or the body twitched. TheHuman was a different matter — he twitched more.

Now in a one-paragraph post, it would be simple enough to put a space in, wherever words are run together. In a longer document (like this entire story) that's just too much of a pain.

We have two choices (notice how I keep breaking things down to two or three choices, that's called *making it simple* and that's my job).

First, we could simply save the word processor file as a plain text file—most software let you do that. This removes the soft returns and saves each paragraph as one long line. These converted files are often hard to proof and edit.

And, to jump ahead a moment, we have another problem in posting long documents. People don't want to be bothered with them unless they are interested in reading whatever you are posting. So we want to post a teaser (short bit of the text) and a link where they can read the whole thing.

Okay, we keeping up? We need to convert the word processing document so that it can be read online, and we need somewhere to put it.

Two word solutions: **Google Docs**. Google Docs is Google's online office suite that's free (if you have a Google account, as you do if you're on Plus). Your documents can be private or shared via links. And, by the way, this also solves posting PDFs and spreadsheets.

It's beyond the scope of this book to show you how to share files, and so on, on Google Docs—but it's darn simple and a great adjunct to your Plus posting.

The following is the actual post for my short story. I use the first two paragraphs as the teaser and the link to the complete 3200-word manuscript on Google Docs.

Again, do the same thing for sharing PDFs and spreadsheets.

Now, let's post stuff already on the web by sharing it on Plus. This, by the way, is the majority of the content you'll see coming by in the Stream. And it's both interesting and entertaining.

Posting from the web

Plus makes all this easy for you—the sharing of web content.

To start with, see something interesting on the web such as Yahoo! News, for example, that you want to share? Just copy the URL (web address), open a post textbox, and paste the URL in. Plus does the rest by creating a graphic, an excerpt, and a link as shown here. Your post is done!

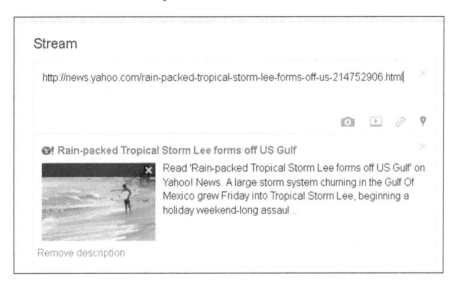

If you drop in a URL and the generated thumbnail photo has arrows in the black band at its top, this means more than one pic is available. Clicking on the left or right arrow shows you other choices.

Clicking on **Remove description** beneath the automatically-generated snippet of the linked site removes the description. Sometimes these are just ads and not appropriate to your link.

Think of posting a link as more than that—consider yourself a magazine editor. After all, Stream is just like short magazine articles flowing by electronically. You have competition vying for the eye of the reader, so a tiny bit of additional effort makes your offering stand out from the others.

I was an editor for a number of years and know it's the little things that grab attention. For example, put in a headline and embolden (asterisks before and after). Grab a paragraph or two as a teaser. (Remember that word from above?)

Be sure to give credit for what you use (such as The Guardian newspaper in the following screenshot). This avoids copyright issues. A snippet of text on a link that pushes people to their site is considered fair usage. Copying a whole article without credit or something in return can get you nasty letters from attorneys.

Here's another enhancement. Before dropping the link in, and on the site being linked to, choose an illustration. Right-click on it and choose **Copy image location** (or however your browser words it).

Now return to your post textbox. Click on the little green camera icon and then select **Add photos** just like we did earlier when uploading a photo from your computer. This pops up a **File Upload** dialog box.

Instead of choosing a picture to upload, click in the **File Name:** box, then press the key combination *Ctrl+V*, which should paste the link of the photo in the box. Click on **Open**. Plus will load the photo from the website and place it nice and big below your article as shown in the preceding screenshot.

The same principle applies to embedding videos in your post, as we see beneath. By the way, this style of posting is one that pleases me; feel free to do it the way that looks best to you.

The trick here, as with photos, is put the video in before putting in the link to the site. Otherwise the Plus system will override you and perhaps include a dinky little thumbnail video instead of the eye grabber you want.

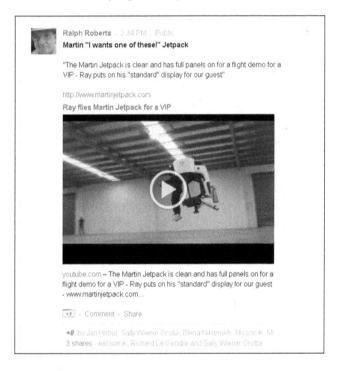

Click on the little red "play" arrow in a box video icon in the post textbox and the following menu appears. We can now upload a video from our computer, from our phone, or from YouTube. As YouTube is owned by Google and integrated into Plus, this is the fastest and simplest way.

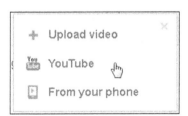

First, find the YouTube video you want to include—like the one about the jet backpack above and copy its URL. Then click on **YouTube** on the preceding menu.

In the dialog box that activates (which we'll examine in detail next chapter) click on **Enter a URL** and *Ctrl+V* the one you copied into the entry box. Click on **Add Video** at the bottom of the dialog box and the video appears nice and large at the bottom of your post.

Finish out the post with headline, teaser, and a link, and then publish it.

Where do you find stuff to post? Most of us check several websites daily. News, sports, travel—all those and more we look at. And lots of sites have interesting things you'd like to share with the circles containing your friends, your co-workers, your relatives, or even just put up publicly for everyone to enjoy or be informed.

And, of course, there are tons of wild and wonderful sites full of trivia, little known historic facts, weird places, cute animals—well, you name it. Lots and lots of stuff to share.

Like this mysterious forest in Poland. People (myself included) find stuff like this fascinating. In the brief time it has been on, this post has garnered eighteen +1s and ten shares (ten people reposted it, giving the article wider exposure). Ten folks commented. The more notice you get, the more followers you attract, and so forth (we cover the benefits of that in *Chapter 7*).

Also, you shouldn't be modest if something nice happens in your life. Like my post today to remind people about one of my previous Packt titles.

Okay, that should get you guys posting more now that we've seen how easy it is and how much fun it can be. However, if we do all these neat posts and they stream on by to wherever they go, how can we save them?

Archiving your posts

To save your posts from the Google+ Stream, go to `https://www.google.com/ takeout`, as follows:

Choose **Stream** and click on **Create Archive** as shown here:

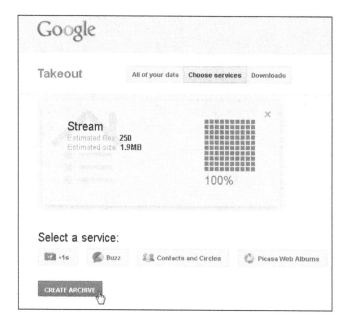

When the posts are found and archived (this is only a copy, the actual posts are left on Plus), click on the **Download** button.

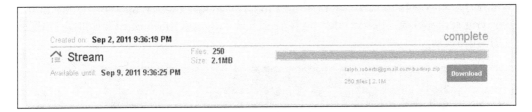

After the download completes, we can open it on our computers and see the posts are saved as separate HTML pages, readable with your web browser.

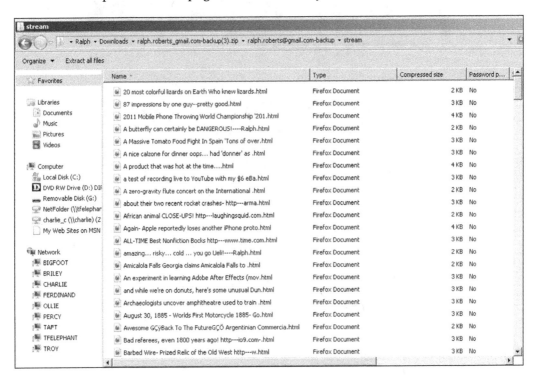

 The limit for archiving posts right now is 250 posts. If you are active on Plus, then you'll want to archive regularly.

Posting from another website

A recently implemented feature allows us to use those ubiquitous (means sprinkled all over the web) +1s to actually post on Plus. If you see a +1 on an article, like in the following screenshot, click on it (you'll need to be logged into your Google account for this to work).

Then click in the **Share on Google+** box.

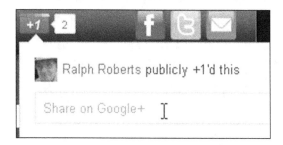

That article will be posted to the Google circles you specify. In the case of the following article, I edited it on Plus to include my comment.

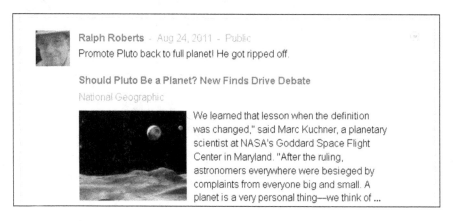

What we learned

We covered a lot in this chapter!

We saw how Stream works, practiced posting, and determined how to drill down so that each post goes to the right audience (by selecting the circle's stream it will appear in). And we learned how to control what we see and when we see it (as opposed to all those zillions of posts you're not interested in, but which make you miss the good stuff on other social networks).

Now, while we were introduced to using pictures, video, and other media in our posts, it's time to explore that universe in more detail—which is all coming up in the next chapter.

5
Sharing Media

In these days of fast Internet connections and ease with which we can share photos and videos we generate and/or find, Plus gives us powerful built-in features for this very purpose.

In this chapter we will be:

- Selecting and preparing photos for uploading
- Uploading and captioning photos
- Using the **Photos** area
- Selecting and preparing videos
- Uploading and captioning videos

Nothing spices up a post like a good illustration and Google Plus makes this easy for us.

Sharing media online indeed has never been so simple. The word **media** refers to methods of communication—not only photographs and video, but also text, audio, and so forth.

Plus has three of the media types mentioned above covered. We'll be examining photo and video in this chapter, and text is when you type and publish your pithy tidbits in the post textbox.

What's missing is audio. I, for one, would love to post podcasts in the form of .mp3 files. A lot of other people—judging by the numbers posting blank videos just to put up a music track—would like that as well. I suspect the ability to include pure audio files will come soon.

Meanwhile, Plus is a powerhouse—as emphasized already—for visually enhancing posts. And that's what we're looking at in more detail in this chapter. First, we need a little preparation.

Preparing photos for Plus

You can upload your photos directly to Google+ without doing anything to them beforehand. The number of photos any one person is allowed on Plus is unlimited.

What is limited is physical size. All photos larger than 2048 pixels on their longest edge get reduced in size to match that parameter. If this does not bother you, then just upload pictures at will.

However, if you want your visual artistry to be the best possible, you might consider storing your photos on something such as **Google's Picasa Web Album** and sharing from there. The size on Plus will still be smaller, but you'll at least have access and can link to full resolution versions of your work.

 By the way, while storage of photos on Plus is unlimited, there is a limit on Picasa of 1GB free storage.

Furthermore, if quality of presentation is important, then you want to enhance color, edit out mistakes, and so on before uploading. For that you need software such as **Photoshop**. Or, if you don't want to spend that kind of money (Photoshop, while the standard image manipulation program, is gosh-awful expensive), there are alternatives such as Photoshop Elements or the open source (free) **Gimp**. See `http://gimp.org`, as shown in the following screenshot, for this free Photoshop-like clone. Additionally, you might want to check **Paint.NET** as another alternative to Photoshop (`http://www.getpaint.net/`).

Yet another solution is using Picasa, Google's free photo editor which, combined with the Picasa Web Albums, is well integrated with Plus. Go to `http://picasa.com` for more information.

Together, as it says on the Picasa site, Picasa and Picasa Web Albums make it easy for you to organize and edit your digital photos, then create online albums to share with friends, family, and the world.

Using the Picasa Web Albums (see following screenshot) is also free. If you already have a Google account (which you do if you're using Plus), then just sign on. If not, then there's a button for creating an account. Additionally, a new version of the Picasa editing software that goes on your computer is available and there's a link on this site to download it.

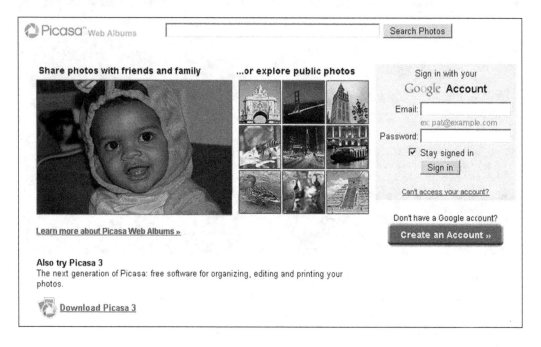

Once you have image editing software (and it's pretty much a necessity), you have more control over how your photography appears once it is online. That alone should be worth the effort.

Picasa, as we saw above, supplies both editing software and a place to store your full resolution photos. This is important as Plus limits the resolution of photos you might display on it.

For example, we now know the 2048-pixel limit for Plus. Instead of relying on the Plus system (which converts umpteen thousand photos at any one time) to treat our photos with loving care, consider resizing and enhancing them yourself so that no conversion occurs.

Use one of the standard formats for still graphics such as .png or .jpg.

Let's do an example of preparation. I found this photo on my system that looked artistic. It has a blackberry bush in focus and Penny the horse (one of two on our farm) artistically unfocused in the background.

Looking at this image in Photoshop, I find it is 4000 x 3000 pixels, certainly above the Plus size limit. Furthermore, the **resolution** (number of dots per inch) at 480 is way too high—wasted on most computer screens, and the color looks a bit washed out.

I change the width to 2048 pixels (the Plus limit) and drop the resolution to 90 dpi (right for most web images). A little on the high end, many of them are just 72 dpi. I also run the **HDR (High Dynamic Range)** and sharpen filters. Now, I have a snazzy image at the maximum size Plus allows.

Opening a post textbox in **Streams,** I click on the little green camera icon and (in the resulting dialog box) find and upload my image. I give it an artsy title and bingo, got a nice post which, judging by the three almost instantaneous +1s, people like.

To be honest, it did not start as art—I took this picture a few years ago just to e-mail my sister that the blackberries were not ripe enough to pick. Now I get to use it as both a post and an example in a book. You never know.

Ah, but the example is not over yet. Click on the photo in the post (or in any post) and Plus expands it out for viewing. Here's the reward! My photo is sized perfectly at the maximum viewing size Plus offers and looks rather nice—much better than relying on the automatic conversion.

Okay, we now look at the ins and outs of uploading and captioning photos and other graphics.

Uploading and captioning Photos

We touched on uploading photographs in the previous chapter, but it's time for a review and some extra detail.

We can upload photos several ways in Plus. These include:

1. Using the small green camera icon in the post textbox, as we did in the preceding section.

2. Clicking on the **Photos** icon on the menu bar at the top of most screens in Plus (see following screenshot). This brings up your photo maintenance section. More about that shortly.

3. Or, as we'll see in a couple of pages, uploading instant photographs from your phone.

To recap the first method, click on **Share what's new...** in any circle's stream, then on the green camera icon as in the following screenshot. This brings up the drop-down menu with its three choices. Choose **Add photos** (we'll examine the other two choices in a moment).

Clicking on **Add photos** opens a file upload dialog box on your computer, as follows:

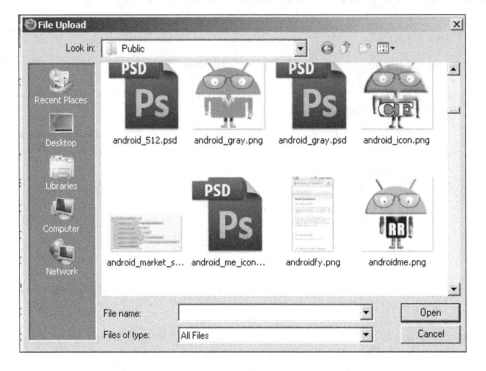

Above, choose the file on your local computer or network to upload. Or paste in the URL to an image on the web. Either way, Plus will insert the photo or other graphic in your post and ask if you'd like to add another. Posts on Plus can have **albums** (a group of related images) of photos, and are not limited to just one photo.

Adding more than one photo to posts

On that drop-down menu we get by clicking on the green camera icon in post textboxes, the second choice is **Create an album**. Albums are groups of photographs and allow us to add more than one photo to posts.

When selected, a dialog box with the following message appears. You can either (using a bit of Web 2.0 JavaScript magic) open a file directory on your computer and simply (using the mouse) drag the photos you want in place. Or click on **Select photos from your computer** and use the **File upload** dialog box we've already made.

As an example, I've dragged in seven screen captures from my *Alien Names* app running on my phone, as shown in the following screenshot:

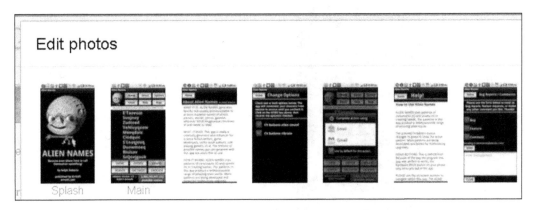

While still on this screen, we can click on each image and caption (add text about what it shows as with **Splash** and **Main** in the preceding screenshot), or delete it.

When we've finished adding photos or graphics for upload, at the bottom of the dialog box are three choices: **Upload more**, **Cancel**, or **Create album**. I'll click on **Create Album** here:

The album appears in the post. In my case, I went ahead and published it on Plus (never waste anything). This promotes my app and people enjoy it (see comments).

Now what if we are out and about and want to call our photos in, so to speak.

Posting photos from your phone

As we saw earlier (if you have the Google+ official app on your phone) uploading photos can be automatic (in the next chapter, I will show you how to turn that off and on). Let me emphasize that these automatic uploads are not public until you share them in a post.

So posting a photo can be done in one of two ways:

1. While using your computer, post a picture from your phone that was uploaded automatically and is now available, stored on Plus.

2. From your phone while away from home. Shoot and post — fast and easy.

As an example of the first method above, I just took a break and walked outside to the pasture fence. When the horses came over in quest for treats, I shot a photo. Now, a couple of minutes later, let's see if we have an automatically uploaded photo to post.

Click on our little green icon in the post textbox, then on **From your phone** in the drop-down menu. This shows the automatic uploads from your phone by date. The one of the hot dogs from Eddie's Dog House was my meal last night—not sure why it didn't come up until today.

 Folks were complaining that my cheap $6 webcam was noisy in **Hangouts** (picture is great). For about $40, I got a Blue Icicle mike preamp and XLR converter that lets me use professional microphones through USB. Everyone loves the sound now.

To finish, choose the photo you want by double-clicking on it to insert in the post, as I did in the following screenshot:

Now, the second method is doing everything from your phone! This does require the Google+ app to be installed. Get it on the main Plus page (bottom of right column) here:

Take the photo or whatever you wish to share on your phone. I did a three-frame panorama from my front yard just after a rain shower. Bring up the menu of your app and choose **Share**.

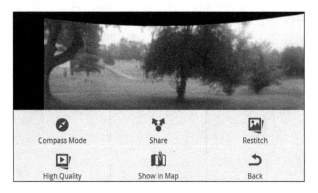

On the list that appears, tap on **Google+**. If Google+ does not appear, then you either do not have the app or it is not installed correctly.

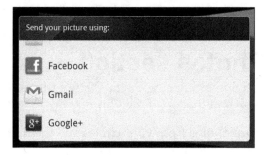

A posting screen appears on your phone. Select the circles for your post, type in a message, let it show your location if you like, then click on the **Post** button (upper-right).

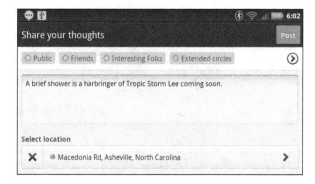

Assuming you have a connection to your carrier's network or by Wi-Fi, the post now appears in the stream on Plus. Mine is as follows:

There are other things you can do on Plus from your phone, but those we'll cover in the next chapter.

Let's now move on to the **Photos** section and look at all the pretty pictures.

Using the Photos section

We access the **Photos** section by clicking on the picture frames icon (second icon from the left in the gray bar at the top of the Plus screen).

The first thing you see are photos from your circles and the first thing you will say is "Huh? Where did all these come from?"

Well, "these" are all the photos, videos, and other graphics posted by people in your circles. Once you have a decent number, there will be literally thousands and they are pretty useless.

It does show who shared them, but generally they are not captioned and you'll have no idea what they are. However, double-click on them and, using the following one as an example, you can do a few things with or to these images.

The **Add tag** button allows you to tag people or objects in the picture with names, should you know them. In this picture, I do not know the name of the kid, the dog, or even the wheelbarrow.

To add a tag (that is, name a person or item in a photograph) click on the photo to enlarge it (a black border appears as shown in the preceding screenshot). Move the cursor over photo and a dashed area with an attached dialog box appears. Put the dashed box over the face or item to be tagged and type the name in the dialog box and hit the *Enter* key to record. You can have as many tags per photo as you like.

In **Actions** above, we can treat ourselves to details about the image (usually sparse) or report an abuse. As an example of abuse, there is the occasional porn picture snuck in by some idiot, but those tend to disappear pretty quickly thanks to abuse reports.

It is possible to share these images, as follows. Just right-click on it, click on **Copy Image Location**, and paste it into the **File Upload** box as you would with any other image from the web.

next, looking in the left column of the **photos** section page, click on **photos from your phone**.

We're already familiar with this page from the last section, when we posted one of those automatically uploaded photos from our phone. This screen shows you what images are available.

The following is how the top of my **photos from your phone** screen looks:

Just above the first row of images are three buttons. When you select an image by clicking on it (a red line around it shows the selection) you can share it (post it), add it to an album (how to do that is coming up), or delete it. Clicking on the name of the album lets you change it.

Next, in the left column, we have **Photos of you**. Or of me on my Plus account, as follows. These are photos that you or someone else has tagged as being you. In the latter case, you may not have uploaded the photo, but it now appears in this category.

Again, to tag any photo anywhere on Plus, click on it. If you get a large version with a black background and there is an **Add tag** button, then you can tag it. Some images are thumbnail links and some images just have the **Photo** and **Report abuse** choices. You just have to try them to see.

Finally, we have **Your albums**. This area should be the most important as it holds all your photos and other graphics. As in mine, shown in the following screenshot, these are albums (collections of photos), not single images. Click on one of these and you should see several other images behind the top one.

When I click on the first photo above (upper-left), I get a new screen showing all the images I've included in recent posts (a lot). Thus, we can find and reuse images.

Having albums of images lets you sort, categorize, and otherwise manage them. Let's take a closer look at albums.

To share any photo in an album, just right-click on it and choose the **Copy Image Location** selection. Paste the link into the **File Upload** box you get through the little green camera icon in the post textbox, just like we've done several times already in this chapter.

On the **Your albums** screen, at the lower-left corner of each album, Plus shows you the album title and the number of photos in it (as follows).

Let's now move on into moving pictures — in this instance, video.

Preparing videos for Plus

Google Plus loves video. Hangouts are a good example — one of the best video conferencing systems around is built right in.

Integration with YouTube is quick and easy to use too.

Additionally, so is uploading your own videos directly into Plus but ... it ... is ... slow. Not through any fault of Plus, but simply because video files are large. Upload times, even for short videos, can be many minutes. Once the video is on Plus, it takes more minutes to encode so it can be shared.

A few things you'll need to know in making sure your video will upload and look its best on Plus. Basically, these are the same limitations as making a video for YouTube, and no wonder, Google owns YouTube and probably uses the same software and hardware to encode video clips.

Size is important — two kinds of size actually. First is the dimension of the frame. Plus has a limit of 1080p — that means 1920 x 1080 pixels, one of the high definition sizes. Most prosumer or higher end cameras shoot this size video, but more and more smaller cameras do as well. I have a pocket-sized JVC cam that does, for example. So this is the largest size you can upload.

Luckily, the majority of phones and small Flip-like cameras shoot 720p or 1280 x 720 pixels.

The other type size is the file size of your video. For years YouTube has limited this to one gigabyte (which is about ten minutes or less timewise). YouTube has recently relaxed this restriction, but Plus so far encourages short videos.

Two ways of preparing your video files for upload:

1. Do nothing to it
2. Edit it using video editing software, enhancing the sound and picture, and adding music and/or voiceovers

While doing nothing is certainly convenient, it is the least desirable. Editing for better sound, cutting out those jerky, amateurish spots, music (helps any video), adding in some voice comments to explain things, and so on literally make you look good.

Many of the editing programs now available have output presets. Choose one for YouTube and you'll have a perfect video, properly compressed to look the best it can on Plus.

Free video editing programs come with both Windows and Macs. Or a simple solution is to upload your video to YouTube and use their new, easy-to-use online video editor.

The main three optimum formats to use for Plus videos are .mp4, .3gp (many phones output this), or .flv (Flash).

Make your video look good before uploading to Plus and it will look good on Plus.

 Plus makes sharing YouTube videos so easy, I recommend putting videos on YouTube first, then sharing them in a post on Plus. This gives you the double advantage of wider coverage for your video on both these highly popular networks, that is, Plus and YouTube.

Uploading and captioning videos

You can upload a video inside the post textbox by clicking on the little video player icon (box with a red arrow in it) but, as noted above, video takes a *loooong* time for uploading and encoding. It is far more convenient to upload it to your Photos area first and then share as a post.

Uploading directly to Plus

Let's look at that process. First, click on the **Photos** icon in the gray bar at the top of the Plus screen, and then click on **Your albums** in the left column of the resulting screen.

You get the **Upload and share** photos dialog box. Click on the blue **Select photos from your computer** button and the **File Upload** dialog appears as follows. I shot a video of the horses, Blaze and Penny and now choose and upload it.

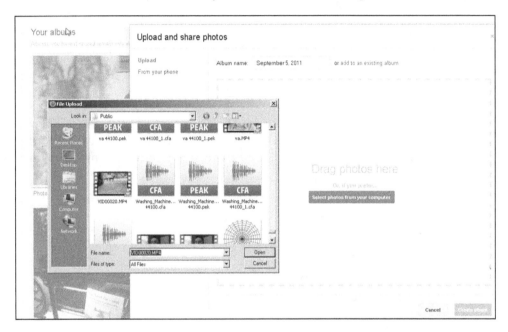

Yes, I hear you. This does look exactly like what we did to upload photographs earlier. Well, it is! Plus knows the difference between a photo and video and we can mix and match them inside albums.

Select a video to upload in the **File upload** dialog.

Again, videos take time to upload. The following progress bar is at the bottom of the first dialog box:

In the dialog box is a grayed out *placeholder* with the video file name and also a progress bar.

Eventually the upload completes and the gray box turns into a black one. Clicking on it allows you to either delete it (not likely after all the time it took) or caption it. My caption is *Blaze and Penny Cavort* as they were acting up and having fun, which is why the video is worth sharing.

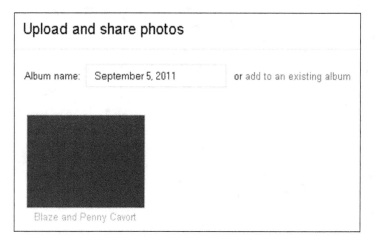

Once you've captioned your video, save it (blue button). It now appears in one of your albums.

In my case, this is the first video or photo I have uploaded today, so it's in an album by itself, shown in the following screenshot. I just click on the **Share album** button and add a bit of explanatory text, and post.

Now, what if the video is on YouTube?

Sharing a YouTube video

Finally, shoot some with your phone and we'll see just how easy it is to include those as well.

Using automatically uploaded videos from your phone

Click on the **Photos** icon (top gray bar) and then on the **Photos from your phone** selection in the left column. I shot two videos on my phone this evening and they are there already.

Click to select a video and you can share it by clicking on the green share button above the videos. Here's what the tropical storm report I shot on my front porch looks like. Thanks to Plus, it's easy to do almost instantaneous news available worldwide.

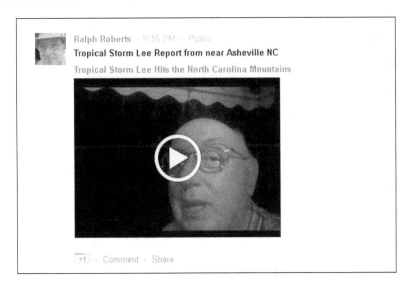

And that's it for photos and videos.

What we learned

In this chapter, we explored selecting and preparing photos for uploading. As Plus relies heavily on visual elements, making the small effort required to enhance photos really pays off.

We then uploaded and captioned some photographs, and played with Actions to tag names of people and items.

We also saw how to use the Photos areas to select and prepare videos, and upload and caption videos.

Now it's time to visit the official (and free) Plus mobile application, then the new Games area.

6
Mobile and Games

In today's world of smartphones, we take our social networks with us, and many of us play games no matter where we are. So, a chapter combining mobile use of Plus and the new **Games** feature seems logical. Here it comes.

In this chapter, we look at:

- Getting the Google+ app for your phone or tablet computer
- Streaming
- Posting from your phone
- How to keep up with Circles, and so on, on the mobile device
- Photos and videos from your phone or other device
- Huddling
- Games on Plus

The Games feature is one of the newest additions to Plus and gives us lots of choices from role-playing games to arcade offerings such as the exceptionally popular *Angry Birds*, as shown in the following screenshot:

But first, let's go all mobile here on Plus.

Getting mobile access to Plus on phones or tablets

We've covered how to get the official Google apps earlier, but here's more on that.

1. Start, of course, by clicking on the **Go mobile** link on the lower-right of the main Plus page after you've signed in (the following screenshot):

2. This takes you to the **Google Mobile** page with those official apps.

3. The quickest way to install an app on your phone or tablet is to go to this link—m.google.com/plus—on your device and tap on the **Send to Phone** button, as shown in the following screenshot:

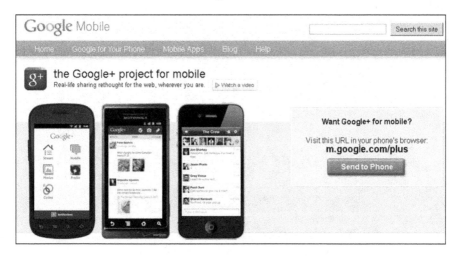

4. The following is the list of supported devices from the preceding site. For full mobile Plus features, you need a later model of either Android or iPhone phones. More limited support is given to Blackberry, Nokia, and Windows phones.

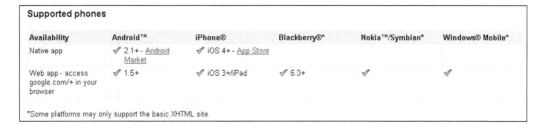

Supported phones					
Availability	Android™	iPhone®	Blackberry®*	Nokia™/Symbian*	Windows® Mobile*
Native app	✓ 2.1+ - Android Market	✓ iOS 4+ - App Store			
Web app - access google.com/+ in your browser	✓ 1.5+	✓ iOS 3+/iPad	✓ 6.0+	✓	✓
*Some platforms may only support the basic XHTML site.					

5. So, we did the preceding procedure when originally installing the app. In my case, going to the mobile site on my Droid 2 and tapping on **Send to Phone**. It worked fine and the following is how it looks on this Android-based phone. Works great too!

6. However, when deciding to add the official Plus app to my tablet computer, I ran into a problem. It asked for my mobile phone number. My tablet (an Android-based device as well), like most, is not a phone — it connects to the net only through WiFi.

7. No problem. Most tablets also have an app that connects to Android Market. Open that, search for Google+, and install the app in that manner.

8. The following screenshot is Plus on the tablet. Much easier to read and comment on posts, and easier to create new posts. Like on phones, photos, and videos can be set to upload automatically, so that they are available for sharing.

9. If you have an iPhone or iPad, the official Google+ app can be found on the iTunes store (free) and the listing looks the following screenshot:

However, what if you don't have a fancy smartphone, but your phone does have SMS (texting)?

SMS only

SMS (short message service) is what makes texting or sending short text messages possible.

If you have an SMS-enabled device, as is stated on the Google Mobile site, then you can subscribe to SMS notifications or use SMS for posting to **Huddle**. (We cover Huddle later in this chapter.)

Just go to the SMS account settings on your phone to enable SMS. Standard message and data rates from your carrier may apply.

Let me emphasize, this is standard texting. You will not need the preceding Google app — just the texting feature already in your phone.

To set up using texting to post, on your computer while logged into Plus, click on the gearwheel settings icon at the far right of the black tool bar across the top of your screen, as shown in the following screenshot. Then, click on **Google+ settings**.

On the settings screen that comes up, you'll need to enter your phone number. At this time, you'll be asked to entered a verification code (which the system texts to your phone). This is for your protection.

Then, check SMS as follows. And that completes the setup.

To send texts, use the number 919-222-222222 in your regular texting app (at least this number works in the United States), as shown in the following screenshot. You can specify a circle or circles by putting the name of the circle behind an at sign (@) and ending it with a period such as @Friends. or @Public. and so on.

Now, back to the official Google+ app as the next several sections explore its various features.

Streaming

Open the Google+ app on your phone and follow along, please.

First, we look at **Stream**. Just like on our computers, it shows the flow of posts. This is its icon:

Tapping on the Stream logo opens the stream. We see posts as in the following screenshot captured from my phone. Scrolling up shows more posts.

Take a closer look at the top menu bar of the **Stream** screen in the following screenshot.

Tapping on **Google+** returns us to the main or start screen of the app.

The checkmark in the white circle is to check in (let selected people know where you are), similar to **Foursquare** and **Facebook Places**. An example would be when arriving at your hotel, use **Check in** to let your family know, or to tip your buds where you're hanging on Friday night.

Here's how that works.

Tapping on it brings up a page of nearby locations. If one fits, then just click on it. Or—as this relies on GPS and only works well when outside with a good sky view of the GPS satellites—we can also search for where we really are. See the following screenshot:

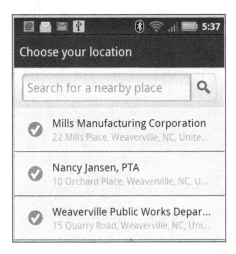

Once a location is selected, we get the posting screen, as follows:

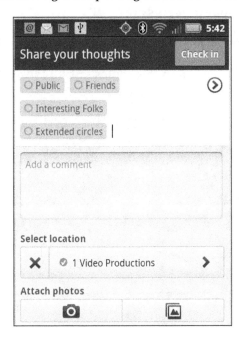

The right-pointing arrow in the circle under the **Check in** button brings up a screen where we can set which circles see the post. Tapping on **Add a comment** brings up the phone's virtual keyboard so we can type in a message such as *Arrived safe* or *Meet me at Joe's*. When we finish, tapping on the blue **Check in** button sends it to Plus.

Hit the hardware **Back** button on your phone or tablet (if it has one) and we return to the **Stream** screen. Clicking the camera icon (shown in the following screenshot) gives us the opportunity to take a photo, or photos (which go into the phone's gallery), or to share up to eight photographs already in the gallery. You might want to take a moment to explore both those options.

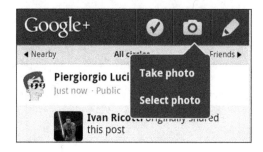

Now look at the pencil icon to the right of the camera in the preceding image. Tap on it and we get the **Share your thoughts** area.

Below the comment area, you can **Attach photos**. The little camera icon takes a picture with your phone and attaches it to the post. The **Photos** icon lets you choose photographs or other graphics from the **Photos** area of Plus, which we saw in the last chapter.

On this screen, use the button in the upper-right to **Post** your message:

Back to the **Stream** screen. The way you choose which circle you're viewing is neat. In the following screenshot, note that **Friends** is now in the middle and the **All Circles** screen has moved out of sight. That's how you change views; just use your finger to slide the screens left or right.

You can control the number of circles on the menu. Get the menu by tapping your phone's menu button and one for the **Stream** screens comes up at the bottom, looking like this:

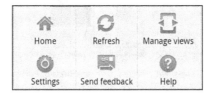

Home returns us to the start screen and **Refresh** refreshes the stream. **Manage views** brings up the following screen, allowing us to choose which views and how many we can see by sliding as we did above. It shows all your circles. Check the ones to be added or uncheck to remove the view. Press the **Done** key when finished.

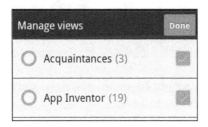

We'll get to **Settings** in a moment. **Send feedback** lets you report issues with the app and **Help** links to online Google documentation.

That finishes our look at **Stream** — back to the start screen, please.

Photos

Tap on the **Photos** icon as follows:

This brings up the **Photos** area of your Plus online account with the same photos, videos, and graphics as you would see from your computer. On our phones, it looks like this:

The camera icon at the upper-right lets you take new pictures with your camera and add them online or select photos to share.

Tapping on the **Google+** icon at the upper-left takes us back to the app's main screen.

Let's check out the Circles feature now.

Circles

The **Circles** feature of the official Google+ app—as with the **Photos** feature we just looked at—is much the same as its counterpart on Plus when accessed from your computer. It's for the maintenance of your circles.

The first screen we get after tapping on the **Circles** icon on the main screen of the app lists our circles. Like elsewhere, tapping on the **Google+** logo (as follows) returns us to the main screen. The **+O** allows us to add new circles to our Plus account.

Clicking on the **People** tab changes the view to people, these being everyone we've added to all our circles. I have almost 5,000 now (that being the current limit of people we can add). It would take some time to scroll through them on the phone.

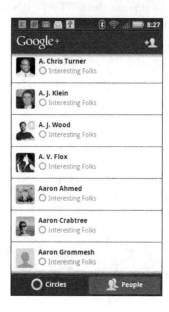

We can drill down into our circles for more detail. Return to the **Circles** tab and tap on your **Friends** circle as I have in the following image. We get a view of the people in that circle. At the top, the logo works as always, returning us to the main screen. More about the speech balloon icon to the right of the logo in a moment.

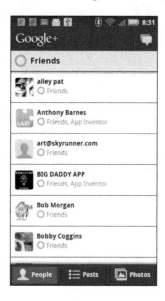

The three tabs at the bottom of the preceding screen are the **People** view (the one being shown), all their posts, and all the photos they've posted respectively.

Clicking on any person gives you a screen with three tabs. These show that particular individual's profile, all his/her posts, and all the photos he/she has posted. As you now see, we can get real details on anyone in any of our circles.

You'll note on the individual screens that same speech balloons icon I promised to reveal. Well, that's to start a **Conversation** with (as the following image). A Huddle (details coming up in the next section) is kind of like two-way tweeting meets online chat.

In our case, if we start it while viewing a circle, then that entire circle gets our messages and can reply. If we start it while looking at an individual, then only he or she will get them and can reply.

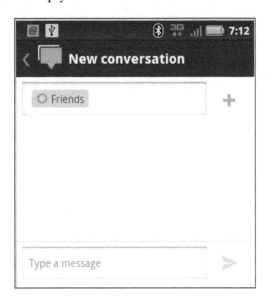

And that gives us the perfect opportunity now of returning to the main screen and tapping on the **Messenger** icon (formerly named **Huddle**) to learn all about messaging!

Messenger

The **Messenger** part of Google Plus is the texting application. You start it from the official Google+ app by tapping on the **Messenger** icon. Although it's started from a phone, people using their computers can receive and respond to texts from **Huddle**. It's also nice to use in **Hangout** for texting back and forth while others are talking.

The first **Messenger** screen that comes up has a record of past and ongoing sessions, like this:

Clicking on any one of them gives you the actual transcript of the conversation that occurred (or is occurring). Not only the messages but also the Profile photos of the huddlers are shown.

The bottom of the screen is the place where you type your messages.

Clicking on any participant lets you view their profile, posts, and photos.

Like the rest of Plus, **Huddle** is both powerful and great fun. Play with it and learn this great communication accessory to the Plus package.

Now, finally on the main screen, it's time to do a bit of profiling.

Profile

The **Profile** icon (that's you looking out at yourself on your phone) shows your profile.

Unlike on Plus from your computer, you can't edit the profile. You can just read it and you probably already know all that stuff. If not, then refer to the profile on your phone. The following one's mine:

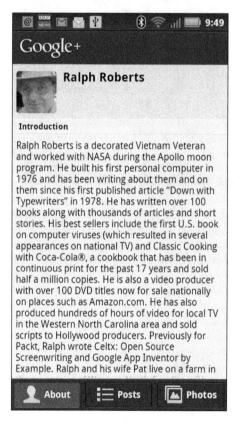

Now, let's check our notifications.

Notifications

We've been introduced to **Notifications** when using the computer to access Plus. You can get notifications through Gmail by clicking the red button in the black toolbar at the top of the Plus main page, or on your phone via the official Google+ app, as follows:

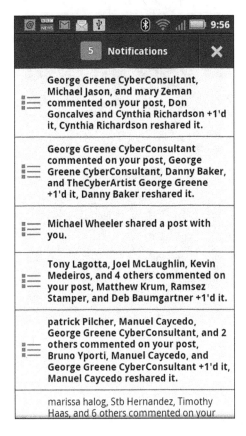

Once your circles become populated, there is a lot going on at any one time. Notifications are how you can keep up.

Finally, in this tour of the Google+ app, we look at settings.

Settings

Tap your phone's menu button and then tap on **Settings**. We get the following screen:

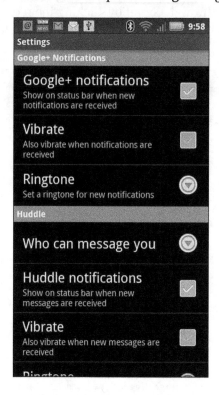

Using the preceding screen, you can customize the Google+ app the way you like.

Now, time for games!

Games on Plus

To visit the **Games** area, click on the **Games** icon (following screenshot) in the gray bar at the top of Plus screens:

The main screen of the **Games** area looks like the following screenshot with a slideshow showing featured games:

Click on the thumbnail beneath the large game graphic to jump to a specific game. Click on the blue **Play** button at the lower-left to play the game featured.

The menu to the left of the screen, under your profile picture, lets you chose **Featured Games** (the first screen you see in this area), a listing of **All games**, and **Game notifications**.

There is also a **Games** stream, as shown in the following screenshot, where players of the various games (that's us) can post comments, questions, offer to trade game stuff, and so on.

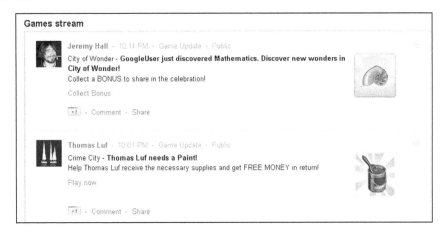

Here is the current **All games** screen. As I write this, Games is still a very new feature. New games are being added all the time, so keep checking back.

And this is the last screen from that menu on the left, the **Game notifications** page (separate from standard notifications).

Playing *Angry Birds*. Look how scared the guy above me looks now that I'm on the scene.

Once I max all the levels of *Angry Birds*, it will be time for *Dragon Age*.

Lots of fun awaiting us in the Games area, that's for sure!

What we learned

In this chapter, we obtained the Google+ app for our phone and/or tablet computer. Then we saw how Stream works on the phone, saw how to post to Plus from a phone, and learned how to navigate our circles.

We also explored how the app lets us manipulate photos and videos, both on our phone and on Plus. Then we jumped right into Messenger and quested our way through a brief overview of Games.

Next comes the chapter on properly promoting on Plus without making people mad at us.

7
Promoting on Plus the Right Way

Many people use social media such as Facebook to promote themselves, their company, their organization, or a cause. Certainly, Plus offers exciting potential for promotion too.

All of this is fine as long as we do it right and don't offend anyone. If people get irritated by your actions, then they won't pay attention to you. If they don't pay attention, then you are wasting your time.

In this chapter, we learn about:

- Netiquette, what it is, and why you should use it
- Marketing politely, but in an interesting manner that works
- The secret of reaching a lot of people on Plus
- Using Plus to promote and drive traffic to your website
- Setting up accounts for a business or organization
- Advertising without it looking like an ad
- Optimizing links to and from Plus
- Starting groups

We'll be looking at all sorts of promotion in this chapter. Here's a tip to start us off. If you have a blog, a company, an organization, a club, or a church website — anything you want people to know about be sure to include the Google +1 button, as I have on my personal blog, as shown in the following screenshot. A good starting point for how to add this button to your site is at `http://www.google.com/webmasters/+1/button/` and most popular blog software, such as Wordpress, offer add-ons to make this even easier (more on that in just a moment).

The marketing done for you by third persons is always the best promotion. When several non-affiliated people are posting items from your sites to Google Plus (and other social media networks), it gives your product or cause more credibility than if you're giving it. This is one of the basic secrets of marketing.

Having such posts appearing regularly (assuming you've put up interesting content that entices surfers into sharing it, now that you've made such sharing easy with those buttons) gets your message out widely. It also drives traffic to your site, sometimes dramatically so.

Add-ons to automatically insert social networking buttons in every post you put on your site are available for most popular content management systems. Wordpress, Drupal, Joomla, and so on, all can be set up to show these buttons. It's a great way to leverage any site!

Here's an example of me promoting my previous book from Packt. I did a time-lapse video (the camera's on briefly every thirty seconds) of myself working on the book. Because of the time lapse, it appears like I write at a blazing pace.

Cute, moderately humorous—people like to share stuff like this. This one I shared myself by posting it on Plus (following screenshot). I just did it as an example for this book. It's been up a little over fifteen minutes, but four people like it, one has shared it (more about that in later parts in this chapter) and Timothy Haas was kind enough to comment on it.

And I like to reply to comments. This does several things for us on Plus, including nice human interaction (the personal touch, retail politics) and it also pushes the post back up in the stream so that more folks see it.

More about all of these concepts and how we can best maximize their use shortly.

Let's discuss online manners (**netiquette**) in general, first—to communicate effectively requires some civility. The Internet, however, is famous for the times it loses civility and users on various forums or mailing lists or, yes, even social networks engage in nasty exchanges—called **flame wars**.

Flame wars start because users hiding behind anonymous aliases sometimes speak their mind, causing others to speak theirs. Much mudslinging ensues. There have been some legendary flame wars in the decades of the Internet and its predecessors.

One of the policies that Google rigidly enforces is the use of real names, discouraging the pseudonyms that lead some to shoot from the lip instead of making reasoned, civil comments. In comparison to many of the places where posts are accepted that I've been on, Plus is a breath of fresh air where people are friendly and there is little nastiness.

Will that stay true as Plus continues growing exponentially? Okay, there will always be some immature dingbat who...oops sorry, got to be civil.

However, seriously, the real name policy really helps. As we've discussed before, Google has a good, strong reason for keeping this policy in place—that being making Plus a source for ID for commerce and all sorts of other reasons. Identity verification is a big bucks business, and Google as well as Facebook and others want it.

Alas (in my opinion) as this book goes to press, Google is relaxing the real name policy.

Anyway, it won't hurt to mention manners. Whether you're marketing something or just communicating for fun, polite interaction keeps things going much smoother.

Netiquette

Netiquette is a code of Internet manners that gives us a guideline of how to correctly do various things online. This concept of codifying virtual civility has been around since the old Usenet days.

A number of guides have been put out, but the one I like best is by my friend Chuq Von Rospach along with Gene Spafford and Mark Moraes, entitled *A Primer on How to Work With the Usenet Community, 1983-1995* (following screenshot). You can read it at: http://www.livinginternet.com/i/ia_nq.htm

> "Netiquette" stands for "Internet Etiquette", and refers to the set of
> practices created over the years to make the *Internet* experience
> pleasant for everyone. Like other forms of etiquette, netiquette is
> primarily concerned with matters of courtesy in communications.
> The following sections provide more information.
>
> - *Netiquette Basics*
>
>   - *Help the newbies*
>   - *Research before asking*
>   - *Remember emotion*
>   - *People aren't organizations*
>
> - *Netiquette Of Sending*:
>
>   - *Be brief*
>   - *Use white space*
>   - *Use descriptive subject lines*
>   - *Stay on-topic*

Netiquette is something not pushed very hard lately. Most Internet users who've started in the last few years have never heard of it.

The lack of common sense with manners on sites allowing anonymous posting today, at times, gets downright spiteful. When no one knows a poster's real name, the use of manners and consideration for the other person get tossed, and profane and disparaging remarks become the rule instead of the exception.

Case in point, several years ago I posted on a local newspaper's site, using my real name. Most of the other posters had screen names (pseudonyms) instead of using their true identity.

The tendency, when I or someone else wrote something they disagreed with, was to insult and tear down the individual they disagreed with. This is called an *ad hominem* attack (which is Latin for "*they'll dump on you personally and not what you said*").

This kind of barbaric behavior runs people off quickly. Me, I sort of enjoyed it. I've been in the Army (where you learn many nifty words) and I have been a professional writer for decades. Mess with me and I can vaporize the case of the attacker's cheap computer and cause his keys to pop off like popcorn with a few well-chosen words.

However, this is unacceptable in polite society, sniping kills honest debate about the issues and no one wins in the long run. Again, this is one of the reasons why Google is so tough on the real name policy. If you're using your real name, then you think twice before publishing uncalled for and insulting posts in reply to someone's opinion.

Personally, I'm all for this. My time on Plus so far has been wonderful. I'm making lots of new friends and reconnecting with old ones. Furthermore, to get back to the topic of this chapter, I'm politely and effectively promoting my books and apps—my two main stocks in trade.

So, please, back to civility. Thank you.

Considerate marketing is effective marketing

The title of this section was originally *Polite Marketing* but that's not totally descriptive. Effective marketing on social media networks goes beyond mere politeness; it requires a good deal of consideration (thinking of all the people reading your posts).

We use social media networks to be, well, sociable. To interact with our friends, with interesting people, learn neat stuff, and receive entertainment.

We do not go on Plus, Facebook or Twitter or anywhere else to read ads. You will note that Google—albeit one of the kings of leverage advertising—does not have ads running up and down the margins of Plus like many sites do. They know better.

Direct advertising—offering a product and pushing for action (that is, a sale)—is not welcome on social networks as it irritates people, and gets you no business.

Being considerate—thinking of others while putting forth your message—does work. If you want to use Plus to promote something, then this is the only way that works. One in which you're giving something of real value to the reader (entertainment) in return for the right to occasionally mention your product, cause, organization, candidate, or whatever.

Don't be single minded in pushing whatever it is you push. Reminds me of what old Fergus Mactavish, a 85-year-old Scot, tougher than nails, who shoots down jets with a rifle and captures a platoon of Marines singlehandedly—one of the characters in my novel, *The Hundred Acre Spaceship*—said. "*Aye, laddie I get yer meaning, ye dinna need to harp on it like some lowland peddler.*"

Far better to show instead of tell. To dribble in a message that builds.

In my case, the main product I have to sell is me. Specifically that I'm an interesting fellow who's done a lot of things, writes great books, produces interesting documentaries, writes useful Android apps, and is a whiz at research. Getting that message out in a subtle yet reinforced marketing campaign that never ceases brings me business. Hey, it's a good living.

So do it nicely and do not harp on it or 10,000 people like old Fergus will gleefully let you know you're doing it wrong.

However, again as this book goes to press, Google is allowing advertising, specifically in now allowing **brand** pages. More about that before this chapter's end.

Content is king

Essentially, content is king. Instead of writing an ad, present interesting and entertaining photos, videos, and (yes) text. If you establish yourself as someone who's contributing and participating and not there to harp on one thing, then you build respect and a following.

The following screenshot is an example (I love getting nice compliments like this). He was responding to an article on copyright (which was not really exciting), but he's commented on several of my posts. It's all part of building your brand online.

 Mark B - You're an interesting man, Ralph. Your research is fantastic. Not necessarily this post; but in general.
10:27 AM   +1

However, let's get back to content.

Luckily, this is not necessarily stuff you have to come up with yourself. We're on the Internet, after all. Linking to fascinating, newsworthy, funny, or informative websites is a time-honored thing. I've done it for years myself.

Why do we do it? Marketing is very much like giving medicine to a dog. Wrap it in something delicious. He'll wolf it down and look to you for more, tail wagging.

Here's an interesting example.

While my publishing company does have several World War II titles, I'm not trying to sell anything here, just entertain. Of course by doing so, I continue to establish my reputation as one who's *an interesting man* and does great research. Eventually, I'll work in a title to sell.

World War II material always has a big following. The following article (my actual post on Plus) has great graphics (this is a visual medium after all), and contains the words *secret*, *wonder weapons*, and *Nazis*. All of these terms guarantee a bunch of people will read it.

Ralph Roberts - 10:02 AM - Public
"Wonder Weapons of World War Two "

DarkRoastedBlend.com - "The Second World War was a period of remarkable advances in technology and many new weapons were invented during this period, some of which entered production and actually saw service in the war, while others never left the drawing board.

"Most of us are familiar with the secret weapons the Nazis had at their disposal in the last months of ...
Expand this post »

+1 - Comment - Share

+6 by Mark B, Ike Davis, Mark A. Sucharzewski and 3 others
5 shares - Claude Martin Brito, David Beck, Ekin Xu, Mohsen Nosrati ...

And, sure enough, people like it. There are six **+1**s, a bunch of comments, and most important of all, five shares!

From a marketing standpoint you really, really want to be entertaining enough to have people share or republish your posts. That means you get your post out to a lot more people than just the ones in your own circles.

A marketing secret

Time to divulge a real secret about the power of Plus in promotional activities. First, look at my profile in the following screenshot. As I write this, I have 4816 members in my circles, which has generated a total of 1215 people adding me to their circles (meaning they can see my posts).

The **Have Ralph in circles** (insert your name) is the only thing that really counts for marketing reasons on Plus. They are the primary viewers of your posts and, as we will see in just a moment, the gateways to a lot more people.

"But, whoa!" you say, *"1215 is pathetic – you can't sell nothing if that's all you're reaching."*

Well, gee, I did that in less than a month and...Okay, I see you are rightly not impressed.

So, here's the secret – **Extended circles**.

Now you might think at first glance, **Public** would be the way to go if you want the widest number possible to see your post. **Public** allows the post to be seen by anyone who's added you to one of their circles, such as my **1215**, or by anyone who views your profile. Nice, but not true Internet power here.

The magic of Extended circles is that a post tagged with it goes to everyone who is in a circle of someone in any of your circles.

Think about it! If my 1215 folks have at least 100 people each in their circles, then 121,500 people can see my posts.

That's actually a very low estimate. I have people following me that have thousands in their circles. There are people on Plus who have hundreds of thousands in their circles. Get a few of those following you and your posts have quite a reach.

The following screenshot is how you tag a post for Extended circles. Click on **Add more people**, and click on **Extended circles** to add it.

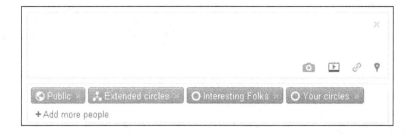

To review, the circles in the preceding screenshot, respectively, allow the following:

- **Public**: The post is seen by anyone who's added you to one of their circles or anyone viewing your profile
- **Extended circles**: Everyone who is in a circle of someone in any of your circles sees the post
- **Interesting Folks**: One of my circles, only people in that circle see the post
- **Your Circles**: Everyone in your circles who's added you can see the post

 If you are promoting several items, then have circles for each item with only you as a member. Include that circle in posts and you'll have a record of the posts in each campaign neatly sorted.

To continue on being considerate: I love finding obscure places, events, people, and so on on the Internet and sharing it. So, I'm not faking anything in what I do and when I work in the occasional promotional item, it's accepted and, often enough even acted on.

In linking to articles on websites, just be sure to honor copyrights by proper usage and attribution. Let me show you one way of doing that.

Here's the formula I like to use when sharing an article (someone else's work) from a website. This formula, while I'm not an attorney, follows the concept of fair usage and attribution and (this one's real important) drives traffic to the linked site, which is what any website wants most.

Refer to the following:

1. Use an emboldened headline to grab attention (remember, use an asterisk to start and end bolded text).

2. Bold the source as with Wikipedia, as follows.

3. Use one or two paragraphs at the most to stay within fair usage (Wikipedia is an exception, it's **Creative Commons** so you can use huge chunks of it but don't try that with CNN for example).

4. Add words like *full article* and the link.

5. Before you add the link, add a photograph or graphic from the site to enhance the appearance (if you wait to do this after adding the link in the posting textbox, you'll find the link pre-empts the photo space and you won't be able to add it).

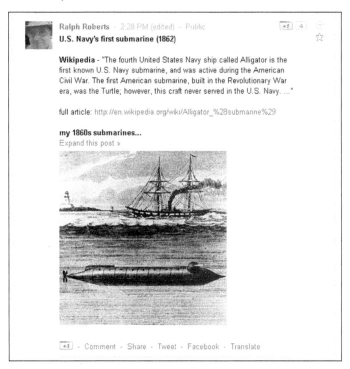

Now, before we go on, there are a few things in the preceding screenshot that we've not seen before. These come from a Google+ extension for **Chrome** (Google's browser). An appendix listing and explaining these extensions is included at the end of this book.

Above, the star lets us bookmark the post. At the bottom of the post, three additional links allow us to tweet, put on Facebook (bet Facebook loves that), or use Google Translate on a post in a language we do not understand.

Develop an editorial sense about what people like and post topics of popular interest. This varies, of course, by the type of audience you're trying to reach. In marketing, we call this **targeting**.

Google Plus right now has a preponderance of high-tech enthusiasts (like me), **first adopters** (those who try out new software or products before their peers), who jumped into the beta, limited membership version of Plus.

And that's fine for what I'm pushing primarily at the moment—computer books, like, say, *Google Plus First Look*. However, I also promote other recent books I've done for Packt—*Celtx: Open Source Screenwriting and Google App Inventor by Example*. Packt offers authors a generous royalty percentage, so it's greatly to my benefit to gently remind people of my books.

Besides, I eat this stuff up. That helps!

Here's another example, an article I found this morning in which the writer presents an interesting analogy about the way Google is developing Android. One guy likes it already.

Now, we're publishing lots of interesting articles, but how do we make sure the maximum number of readers possible are being exposed to them?

Maximizing article views

As we discussed earlier, using Extended Circles makes your posts visible to all the people who have you in their circles and all the people in their circles.

If you have built your **Following** (people who have you in their circles) up to a thousand (as in our example), then that can easily be over 100,000 readers. Newspapers, magazines, and big websites spend megabucks to get that kind of readership, but it is yours for free on Plus.

However, the problem we have is this post is among thousands of others whizzing by in the public **Stream**. If someone has several thousand people they're following, then *whizzing* is the proper term. Articles come up and before you can finish reading them, others have pushed it out of sight.

 For people whose posts you really enjoy (mine?), create a circle with just them in it. That way their posts are accumulated and you can read them at your leisure, not missing any.

Here's the solution to getting your article seen many times and during various times, day and night. Simply comment on it and thereby encourage others to comment too. Every time one of your posts gets a comment or a **+1** (someone likes it), it gets pushed back up in the stream.

In the following post (on the 1860s sub in Panama) my comments encourage others to comment:

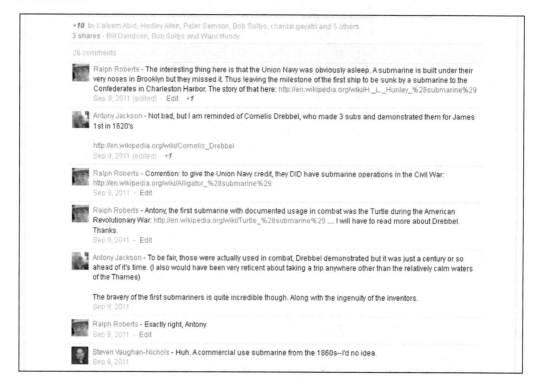

Another way to up viewers is by external links in mailers, posted on other websites, and so on. To get the external link (called a *permalink*), click on the **Options menu** button at the upper-right of all your posts (seen if you are logged in). Then, choose **Link to this post**.

Now you have a post (like mine in the following screenshot) that the general public can see, even if they are not members of Plus. Copy the link from the URL window of your browser and you can paste it in e-mails, on forums, and so on. If they are a Plus member, then they can comment on it or **+1** it.

If you have a blog or other website—pretty much a necessity for marketing on any long-term basis, then be sure to provide links to your posts on Plus.

The following is my personal blog, http://ralphroberts.net (drop by and check me out). On it, to increase interest and traffic, I repost some of my articles from Plus, which always have links back to the article on Plus, then to the rest of the material. This serves a twofold purpose of exposing people to my Plus streams as well as the content twice (redundancy, one of the secrets of good marketing).

Furthermore (in the lower right) I have a listing of my most recent posts on Plus and links to them, as well as (the red and white button) a way to add me to their circles for Plus members. This site is WordPress and there are several plugins already available to tie your blog to Plus so that stuff like listing the recent articles are automatic. However, other content management systems have these add-ons too.

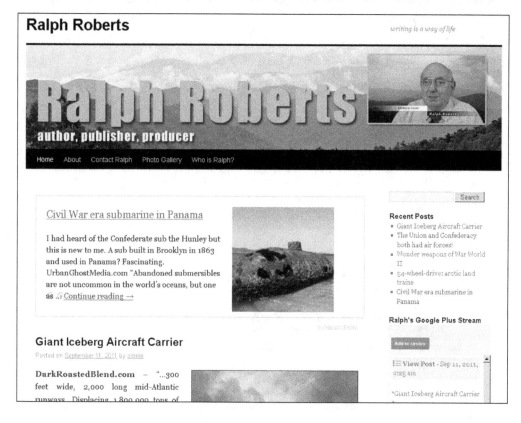

One more good thing about posting on Plus. Google recently (as I mentioned in an earlier chapter) made the contents of Plus visible to the Google (and other) search engines. So, people just doing web searches can find your content.

Furthermore, you might want to consider (if you need a blog site) Google's free Blogger service (`http://blogger.com`). As I write this, several major enhancements are underway to integrate Blogger-hosted blogs with Google+.

Driving visitors to your website

The preceding section was about pushing people to your posts on Plus. This one's about driving folks to your website(s).

The first thing you want to do is make sure that in the upper-right of the **Edit Profile** page you've entered the websites you want to promote, as I have in the following screenshot. Choose **Anyone on the web** for who can see them (bottom, above the **Save** button). This makes sure that search engines can find your profile, thus anyone using those search engines can see you.

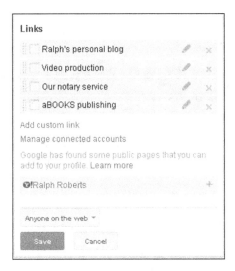

Don't forget to include links in your posts. Develop a pithy signature to add to all your posts (something I have to do too).

Here's what came up for me, searching on Google. As I'm logged into Google, I see an **Edit profile** button as well. All this is another example of how (as also mentioned earlier) Google ties Plus into all its other services. Google+, as has been stated by Google, is considered an extension of Google, not a separate service.

For the above to work, click on the blue and white button to edit your profile and scroll all the way to the bottom of the pages, to the button that sets who can see your profile. Put a check in the box **Help others find my profile in search results**.

Okay, so far you've perhaps noted I've been doing all of these things in my personal Plus account. What about business accounts?

Business and organization accounts

Short answer to business accounts, not yet. Plus does not allow business pages or business names as members yet.

It's a pretty safe bet that once Google Plus is fully open to the public, business accounts will be enabled. For now, we have to do the workarounds as we have been looking at in this chapter.

Starting circle groups

However, what you can do is start groups for each marketing campaign or each interest you might have. I see this happening on Plus already. It's simple. Create a circle for your group. Invite people into it. They create a circle on their end and invite the other members of the circle. You now have a group where everyone in the group sees everyone else's posts.

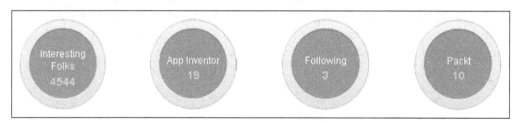

Now, something brand new just before press time!

Google+ pages

From its opening, there has been pressure on Google to provide the ability for businesses, celebrities, and others to create brand web pages on this fast-growing social network. This past week, just as we finish proofing this book, those *brand* pages became a reality.

As a member of Google Plus, you can have as many brand pages as you like. On the main Streams screen, look at the bottom-right, below hangouts (see following illustration). Click on **Create a Google+ page** to add a page:

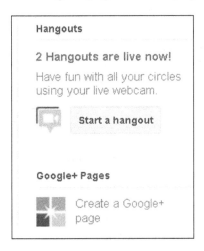

Once the page (a simple process like you're already using on your regular profile) is created, a drop-down menu appears next to your profile picture on the Streams screen. Choose **You** to be yourself or the name of a page to edit your branded page or pages. In the following screenshot, I've added a branded page of this book to my account:

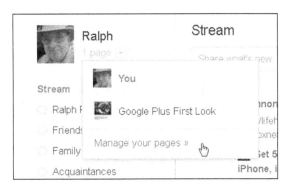

Here is what that page looks like:

While editing your page or pages, you can promote it by using the **Spread the word** feature at the bottom-right of the page.

Google+ pages are less than a week old with few features so far. However, we can count on more and more powerful ways of marketing to be added. It's an exciting time to be learning how Google Plus works!

What we learned

In this chapter, we looked at netiquette, what it is, and why you should use it. We found that marketing politely but in an interesting manner works, and that the secret of reaching a lot of people on Plus is **Extended circles**!

We explored using Plus to promote and drive traffic to our websites and learned that setting up accounts for a business or organization is not yet available.

Throughout all of this, we determined that content is king and that it is the best way to advertise without it looking like an ad. We also mastered how to optimize links to and from Plus, and start groups.

Conclusion

Let me sum up why I like Google+ so much over...oh, say, Facebook.

In something over four years on FB, I've amassed 451 friends. If I do an update on FB, then there is the possibility that 451 people will see it (less, of course, in reality, as people come and go).

In a mere three months on Plus, I have (as of now) 9,838 followers (people who have added me to their circles).

By posting using Extended circles, my posts can be read by not only my own 9,838 followers but all their followers too. If they only average 100 followers each (but I suspect it's a lot more than that) then 9,838 multiplied by 100 is 983,800 people! Is that better than 451? Yep.

That's why I'm on Plus.

And this completes our book except for a few pages in the *Appendix*. There I'll give you some useful web links to better use Plus, and a look at extensions to enhance Plus for users of Chrome.

Thank you for buying and reading my book. It's been an honor to inform and (I hope) entertain you a bit in these pages. All the best and see you on Plus!

— *Ralph Roberts*

Appendix

Here is some additional information that may prove useful in your mastery of Google Plus: third-party websites and useful extensions running on Google's Chrome and other browsers.

Third-party websites

Google has yet to widely release the **Application Programming Interface (API)** to Google+, but there are still third-party (not associated with Google) sites that enhance using Plus. The following are a few of these sites:

FindPeopleOnPlus.com: A directory site indexing over sixteen million Plus users now and ranking the top people. Mark Zuckerberg, a founder of Facebook, ironically has more followers than Larry Page and Sergey Brin, both founders of Google. Check it out at `http://findpeopleonplus.com`.

SocialStatistics.com: Indexes even more folks on Plus. Note Mark's got over half a million followers here:

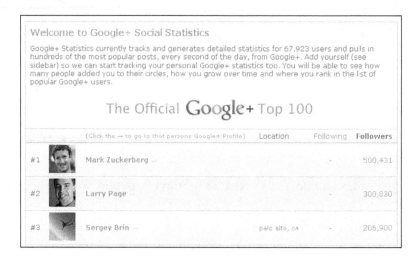

This site ranks all of us. Good for the ego (if naught else) to see I rank 5,107th out of over 32 million, that's not bad.

You can find your own rank at `http://socialstatistics.com/` once you've registered to be tracked.

GooglePlusSearchEngine.com: A search engine just for Plus. Find it at `http://www.googleplussearchengine.com/`.

I like this site because it searches posts when I need to find something from mine or others' posts. It's supported by ads, so you'll see some of those occasionally.

PlusHeadlines.com: This site collects articles about Google+ and is a handy place to keep up with the latest news. In fact, I just learned two pieces of news from the site as this is written.

First, the stream jumping issue is being fixed this week! I mentioned that to you back in the book, where (when you have lots of people in your circle) the stream jumps on you (because of new posts flowing in) before you can finish reading the article you're looking at. Very annoying, and I'm glad to see the fix coming so quick.

Second is Ford Motor Company is being allowed to do a test on Google. And there are other indications (according to the article) that roll out of business pages is imminent on Plus. Commercial activity is good and bad. Good in that the more revenue Google gets, the better they will support Plus and the more goodies we users get. Bad in that there will be ads, but that's life.

To visit this site, go to `http://plusheadlines.com`. I think it's worth a bookmark.

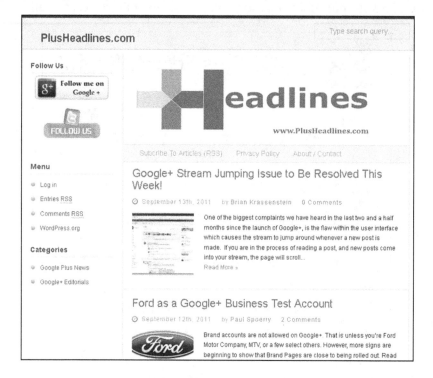

Extensions

Extensions, add-ons, and plugins are all extras we add to our browsers to enhance using Plus.

There's not much out there yet for Firefox and Internet Explorer. Chrome, as might be expected as it is also from Google, has a number of extensions for Plus.

One extension that is available for all of the preceding browsers—*Search for Google Plus*—you will definitely want. Get it at `http://googleplussearch.chromefans.org/` (see following image).

What this extension does for Firefox is add a specialized search engine to your search box on the upper-right of the browser, which you can choose to use in the drop-down menu shown in the following screenshot:

Thus, if I search for *panama sub* I get my article about the 1860s sub used for pearl fishing in Panama. Searching posts in Plus is currently easier with this third-party add-on.

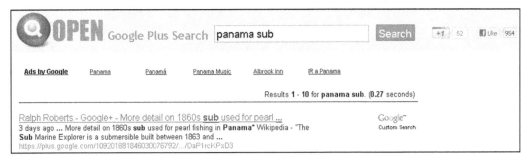

For Internet Explorer, also go to `http://googleplussearch.chromefans.org/` and click on the link to install. You'll get the following dialog box. Just click on **Add**.

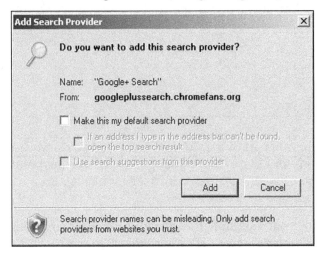

You can now click on the downward arrow next to the URL box and get a specialized Plus search.

And it's also available as an Android app, which looks like the following image, on your phone:

In Chrome (Google's own browser), *Search for Google Plus* is installed like the preceding image.

And, by checking available extensions as you normally would, you'll find *Helper for Google+*, as shown in the following screenshot. This is the extension I showed you in *Chapter 7, Google+ on Your Mobile Device*, which adds bookmarks, Google Translate, and the ability to tweet, and send the post to Facebook. Very worthwhile having!

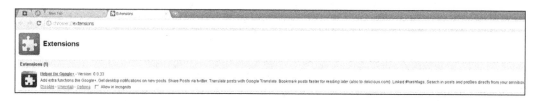

As Chrome and Plus are part of the Google family and so closely associated, more and more extensions for Plus are popping up. A good starting point for more extensions is: `http://smashinghub.com/10-chrome-extensions-for-extremely-amazing-google-plus-experience.htm`

That's it. Thanks for your attention. Please add me to your circle on Plus for continuing tips and entertainment. Happy *plussing*!

Index

Thank you for buying
Google Plus First Look: a tip-packed, comprehensive look at Google+

About Packt Publishing

Packt, pronounced 'packed', published its first book "Mastering phpMyAdmin for Effective MySQL Management" in April 2004 and subsequently continued to specialize in publishing highly focused books on specific technologies and solutions.

Our books and publications share the experiences of your fellow IT professionals in adapting and customizing today's systems, applications, and frameworks. Our solution based books give you the knowledge and power to customize the software and technologies you're using to get the job done. Packt books are more specific and less general than the IT books you have seen in the past. Our unique business model allows us to bring you more focused information, giving you more of what you need to know, and less of what you don't.

Packt is a modern, yet unique publishing company, which focuses on producing quality, cutting-edge books for communities of developers, administrators, and newbies alike. For more information, please visit our website: www.packtpub.com.

About Packt Enterprise

In 2010, Packt launched two new brands, Packt Enterprise and Packt Open Source, in order to continue its focus on specialization. This book is part of the Packt Enterprise brand, home to books published on enterprise software – software created by major vendors, including (but not limited to) IBM, Microsoft and Oracle, often for use in other corporations. Its titles will offer information relevant to a range of users of this software, including administrators, developers, architects, and end users.

Writing for Packt

We welcome all inquiries from people who are interested in authoring. Book proposals should be sent to author@packtpub.com. If your book idea is still at an early stage and you would like to discuss it first before writing a formal book proposal, contact us; one of our commissioning editors will get in touch with you.

We're not just looking for published authors; if you have strong technical skills but no writing experience, our experienced editors can help you develop a writing career, or simply get some additional reward for your expertise.

Google App Engine Java and GWT Application Development

ISBN: 978-1-84969-044-7   Paperback: 480 pages

Build powerful, scalable, and interactive web applications in the cloud

1. Learn how to create realistic game worlds with Google's easy 3D modeling tool

2. Populate your games with realistic terrain, buildings, vehicles and objects

3. Import to game engines such as Unity 3D and create a first person 3D game simulation

4. Learn the skills you need to sell low polygon 3D objects in game asset stores

Google SketchUp for Game Design: Beginner's Guide

ISBN: 978-1-84969-134-5   Paperback: 300 pages

Create 3D game worlds complete with textures, levels and props

1. Learn how to create realistic game worlds with Google's easy 3D modeling tool

2. Populate your games with realistic terrain, buildings, vehicles and objects

3. Import to game engines such as Unity 3D and create a first person 3D game simulation

4. Learn the skills you need to sell low polygon 3D objects in game asset stores

Please check **www.PacktPub.com** for information on our titles

Google App Inventor

ISBN: 978-1-84969-212-0   Paperback: 356 pages

Create powerful Android apps the easy all-visual way with Google App Inventor

1. All the basics of App Inventor in plain English with lots of illustrations

2. Learn how apps get created with lots of simple, fun examples

3. By an author with over 100 books, who keeps it entertaining, informative, and memorable. You'll be inventing apps from the first day

Google Apps: Mastering Integration and Customization

ISBN: 978-1-84969-216-8   Paperback: 268 pages

Scale your applications and projects onto the cloud with Google Apps

1. This is the English language translation of: Integrer Google Apps dans le SI, copyright Dunod, Paris, 2010

2. The quickest way to migrate to Google Apps - enabling you to get on with tasks

3. Overcome key challenges of Cloud Computing using Google Apps

4. Full of examples and including a case study: 'Advanced integration with information systems'

Please check **www.PacktPub.com** for information on our titles